best hikes with
dogs

LAS VEGAS & BEYOND

best
hikes
with
dogs
LAS VEGAS & BEYOND

Kimberly Lewis &
Paula Jacoby-Garrett

THE MOUNTAINEERS BOOKS

Dedication

For you, JJ. Your spirit will always hike on with me.
—KSL

For Mom and Dad, thanks for telling me I could do anything.
—PJ

THE MOUNTAINEERS BOOKS
*is the nonprofit publishing arm of The Mountaineers Club, an organization
founded in 1906 and dedicated to the exploration, preservation, and
enjoyment of outdoor and wilderness areas.*

1001 SW Klickitat Way, Suite 201, Seattle, WA 98134

© 2005 by The Mountaineers Books

Published simultaneously in Great Britain by Cordee, 3a DeMontfort Street, Leicester,
England, LE1 7HD

Manufactured in the United States of America

Acquiring Editor: Cassandra Conyers
Project Editor: Laura Drury
Copy Editor: Carol Poole
Cover and Book Design: The Mountaineers Books
Layout: Mayumi Thompson
Cartographer: Moore Creative Designs; Profiles: Judy Petry
Photographer: All photos by authors unless otherwise noted.

Cover photograph: *With her pack, Camy enjoys a summer hike at Mount
Charleston.*
Frontispiece: *Stoney has been hiking the Mojave Desert since he was a pup.*
Photo by Alex Heindl.

Maps shown in this book were produced using National Geographic's *TOPO!*
software. For more information, go to *www.nationalgeographic.com/topo.*

Library of Congress Cataloging-in-Publication Data
Lewis, Kimberly S.
  Best hikes with dogs. Las Vegas and beyond / Kimberly S. Lewis & Paula M. Jacoby-
Garrett.-- 1st ed.
      p. cm.
  Includes bibliographical references and index.
  ISBN 0-89886-990-0
  1. Hiking with dogs--Nevada--Las Vegas Region--Guidebooks. 2. Trails--Nevada--Las Vegas
Region--Guidebooks. 3. Las Vegas Region (Nev.)--Guidebooks. I. Jacoby-Garrett, Paula M.
II. Title.
  SF427.455L49 2005
  796.51'09793'135--dc22
                              2005007565

 Printed on recycled paper

CONTENTS

Red Rock Canyon National Conservation Area

Spring Mountains National Recreation Area (Mount Charleston)

Valley of Fire State Park

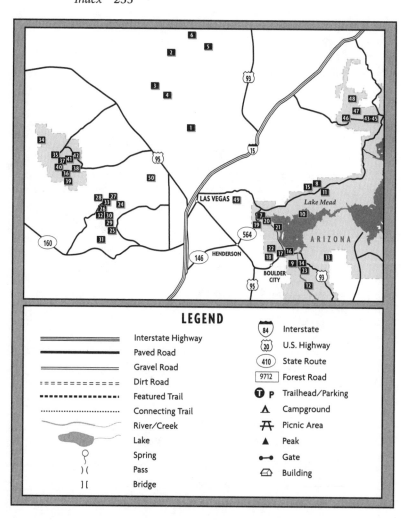

LEGEND

Interstate Highway	
Paved Road	
Gravel Road	
Dirt Road	
Featured Trail	
Connecting Trail	
River/Creek	
Lake	
Spring	
Pass	
Bridge	

84	Interstate
20	U.S. Highway
410	State Route
9712	Forest Road
T P	Trailhead/Parking
△	Campground
⅄	Picnic Area
▲	Peak
●—●	Gate
⬠	Building

HIKE SUMMARY

	Up to 5 miles	Over 5 miles	Water (S=seasonal)	Swimming	Shade	Rock scrambling	Backpacking	Good for senior dogs	Best for fit dogs	Shorter hike distance is possible	with 4wd or two cars
Desert National Wildlife Range											
1. Gass Peak		•	S			•		•	•		
2. Hidden Forest		•	•		•		•		•		
3. Joe May Canyon		•	•						•		
4. Long Valley		•			•				•		
5. Mormon Well	•	•			•			•			
6. Sawmill Canyon		•	•		•		•		•		•
Lake Mead National Recreation Area											
7. Bluffs Trail	•							•			
8. Bowl of Fire		•	S			•					•
9. Boy Scout Canyon		•			•	•			•		•
10. Callville	•			•	•						
11. Cottonwood Spring	•				•			•			
12. Crane's Nest Rapids		•	•	•	•	•					•
13. Horsethief Canyon		•	S		•	•					•
14. Liberty Bell Arch	•									•	
15. Lovell Canyon		•			•	•					•
16. Railroad Tunnel Trail	•					•		•			
17. Reverse Railroad to Knoll	•							•			
18. River Mountain Trail		•									
19. River Mtns Loop—Segment 17	•							•			•
20. River Mtns Loop—Segment 18		•						•			•
21. Sunset View	•			•	•			•			
22. Teddy Bear Cholla Forest	•										•
23. White Rock Canyon	•			•	•						
Red Rock Canyon National Conservation Area											
24. Calico Tanks	•		S			•					
25. First Creek	•		S	•							
26. Ice Box Canyon	•		S		•	•			•		
27. Keystone Thrust	•										

	Up to 5 miles	Over 5 miles	Water (S=seasonal)	Swimming	Shade	Rock scrambling	Backpacking	Good for senior dogs	Best for fit dogs	Shorter hike distance is possible with 4wd or two cars
28. La Madre Spring and Cabin	•		•		•	•				•
29. Oak Creek Canyon	•				•	•				
30. Pine Creek Canyon	•		S		•	•				
31. Rainbow Springs to Bootleg Spring		•	•		•			•		•
32. Red Rock Escarpment	•				•	•			•	
33. White Rock–LaMadre Spring Loop		•	•		•					
Spring Mountains National Recreation Area (Mount Charleston)										
34. Bonanza Trail (Spring Mountains Divide Trail)		•	S		•		•		•	•
35. Bristlecone Loop		•			•				•	•
36. Cathedral Rock	•		S		•				•	
37. Cave Spring via Trail Canyon	•		•		•					
38. Fletcher Canyon	•		S		•	•				
39. Griffith Peak via Harris Springs Road		•			•		•		•	
40. Mary Jane Falls	•		S		•					
41. Mummy Springs		•	•		•					
42. North Loop Trail at Hwy 158 to Trail Canyon Trail		•	•		•				•	•
Valley of Fire State Park										
43. Arrowhead Trail	•							•		
44. Charlies Spring and Beyond		•	•			•				
45. Natural Arch	•									
46. Pinnacles	•									
47. Rainbow Vista Trail with a side trip to Fire Canyon Overlook	•							•		
48. White Dome Loop	•				•	•		•		
Other Areas										
49. Frenchman Mountain	•								•	
50. Lone Mountain	•								•	

ACKNOWLEDGMENTS

We would like to thank all the people who helped us prepare this book. Their help and encouragement have been tremendous. First, we would like to thank our families for their support. Dinah, Jeff, Barb, Doug, Tracy, Lisa, George, Sylvia, Bill, Gwen, and Evan—thanks for putting up with us! We also thank all of our friends who let us drag them (and their dogs) out hiking weekend after weekend, particularly Kristi Johannes.

Quite a few people offered us help by sharing expertise in the fields in which they specialize. Thank you, Dr. Diaz and all the veterinarians and staff at the Pebble Maryland Animal Hospital, for your great advice and the care of our dogs (and many of the other dogs pictured in the book). We also found the input from Alex Heindl, Linda Lane, Kathleen Miller, Tracy Lewis, Beth Tomica-Hewitt, Ryan Hewitt, and Ed Remington extremely helpful. Last but certainly not least, we would like to thank the federal and state employees at the Bureau of Land Management, Desert National Wildlife Range, Lake Mead National Recreation Area, Spring Mountains National Recreation Area, and the Valley of Fire State Park for helping us select appropriate hikes and ensuring that the information within their jurisdictions was current and appropriate.

PART 1

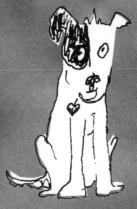

Hiking Tips for Dogs and People

*"The most important role of dogs today is to
be our friends and companions. Dogs require loving
attention, but they give back more
than they receive."*

—Dorothy Hinshaw Patent (Dogs: The Wolf Within,
Lerner Publishing Group, 1992)

Enjoying the outdoors is a way to relax, exercise, and get rid of stress. Bringing our faithful companion along is like having a comrade on the trail, someone to appreciate the glorious and unique desert environment with us. The following information is a guide to hiking safely and providing the most rewarding experience possible on the trail.

Good Dogs Require Good Owners

Since 8000 BC, there have been domesticated dogs. These ancestors of the wild, with their variations in size and color, all have one thing in common: their allegiance and loyalty to humans. They have been dedicated companions, soldiers in war, helpers on the farm, and assistants to the handicapped. Their love and compassion for their owners is so strong, they deserve the best of everything we have to offer them.

The decision to acquire a dog, however, is one that shouldn't be taken lightly. Although dogs can be loving, protective companions, there is a great responsibility to having and caring for a dog. Our responsibility as good dog owners is to maintain our pets' health and sufficiently train our pets to be well-behaved members of society. In fact, there is no substitute for a well-trained dog. At home or on the trail, a well-behaved pooch is essential for a rewarding experience and relationship. Dogs need to be trained to be social with other dogs and people, and to be responsive to commands. These traits not only show off your pooch as a well-trained animal but also serve to keep your pet safe. Training is also crucial for those dogs that may never be social and comfortable with other dogs, or children. Understanding your dog's social needs and limitations, and having a good training background, will teach you how possible problems can be avoided or controlled.

To protect yourself as well as your pet, follow the law when it comes to licensure and vaccinations. Dogs are required to be vaccinated against rabies, and to carry their rabies tag. Dogs should also have a dog license as per your city's requirements. Having an identification tag and/or microchip for your pet increases the probability that you will be able to find your pet if lost. If visiting from another area, have a temporary address and phone number on your pet's tag to ensure you can be contacted. Having a photo readily available will also assist authorities in finding your pet, if lost.

If a dog bites another dog or a person, it is the responsibility of the dog owner(s) to provide the injured party with the dog's license and rabies information as well as the owner's name and address. If the situation is serious, contact the appropriate authorities.

Another responsibility of a dog owner is to neuter male dogs and spay female dogs. Frequently after two years of age, male dogs will try to assert their dominance over other dogs. Neutering them reduces this inclination and their tendency to roam. Female dogs in season should never be taken on the trail. Instinctively they will be more competitive with other female dogs, and be distracting for male dogs in the area. For both males and females, instincts and hormones can override obedience classes. Neutering or spaying your dog will greatly reduce the chance of conflicts with other dogs on the trail.

Dr. Diaz gives Dean a general health checkup.

Myths and Misunderstandings about Dogs

These are some common and easily disproved myths about dogs on trails:

Small dogs cannot hike. Originally, dogs were bred to perform a particular function such as herding, security, or getting rid of varmints. Dogs in general were bred to be active members of a household. Today, some breeds may typically be thought of as housedogs, but they too enjoy the activity and, even more so, the mental stimulation that a new and different environment gives them.

Take the breed's physical characteristics into account when determining which hike to take. For example, the long body of dachshunds and bassets makes them more susceptible to back injuries. For these dogs, a trail with a lot of jumping and climbing may not be appropriate. The Doberman pinscher is typically a lean dog with little body fat, which can make this breed chill easier in water or cold-weather environments. No matter the breed, your pet can become a hiking dog if you stay within its physical limitations. "Even the tiniest poodle or Chihuahua is still a wolf at heart." (Dorothy Hinshaw Patent, *Dogs: The Wolf Within*, Lerner Publishing Group, 1992.)

Dogs should not be on trails. Unfortunately, some irresponsible

Good trail etiquette means leaving only paw prints.

pet owners have made a bad rap for our four-legged companions. Some view dogs as a nuisance on the trail, leaving waste everywhere, running up to people and jumping up on them, etc. A well-trained and picked-up-after pet can be a great joy to have on the trail for the owner, and does not have to ruin another's hiking experience. The only way to get this bad rap remedied is by cleaning up our act, literally, and making sure our pets are the wonderful additions to society we see them as. Remember, it is a privilege to have dogs on the trail. The majority of National Parks do not allow dogs on trails.

Dogs cause damage to the fragile desert environment. There is no doubt that the desert is a fragile environment. Dogs can damage a pristine desert landscape, just as people can. The hikes included in this book are on established trails. They have been created for recreational activities and are meant to withstand the wear of hikers' boots. By staying on established trails, dogs and people enjoy the wonders of our desert environment without damaging it. Cleaning up pet waste eliminates the impact the nutrient-rich deposits can have on our sensitive environment.

Good Canine Trail Etiquette

On the trail you are responsible for your dog's actions as well as your own. Be courteous and thoughtful of others on the trail. Yield to other users on the trail. Those hiking uphill have the right of way on a trail; if heading downhill, step off trail and let the others pass.

Respect other visitors and protect the quality of their experience. The majority of people on the trails are looking for beautiful scenery, fitness and solitude. Respect others and don't impose your presence on their nature experience.

Not everyone is a dog lover or is comfortable with dogs. Allowing your dog to run freely up to other people or jump on them could be traumatic for those who are unfamiliar with canine companions.

Maintain control of your pet. There are many opportunities for obedience training in the greater Las Vegas area. Obedience classes are available at local pet stores, the University of Nevada, the Community College of Southern Nevada, and from many private trainers. Whether you are taking a class or training your dog on your own, there are several commands that are helpful if you plan on hiking with your pup. "Stay," "come," "down," "heel," and "sit" are the usual commands your dog will learn. Another command, "off trail," is useful for encountering other trail users. The command tells your dog when to get off the trail and allow others to pass. "Leave it" is also a helpful command. Dogs will often find an item on the ground before we get a chance to determine if it's something they should be playing with, sniffing, rolling in, or eating. When you give the command, your dog should walk away from the object, which will allow you the opportunity to find out what the item is.

> *"Dogs love to roll in obnoxious organic material because they have a highly evolved sense of smell, probably a million times better than ours, and I believe that they have an esthetic sense in this modality: they like to wear odors much as we, a more visually oriented species, like to wear bright clothes or something different for a while."*

> —*Michael W. Fox* (Superdog: Raising the Perfect Canine Companion, *Howell Books, 1990)*

Always clean up after your pet on the trail. This is one of the main complaints from people who are opposed to allowing dogs on trails. By always cleaning up after your pet, you will win a point for those of us who love hiking with our dogs. If you find it disgusting to pack the waste out, one trick is to store it in your dog's pack. Clean up the waste with a doggie bag and then place it in either a bag that seals at the top or a disposable plastic container. This ensures that the aroma is contained. Finally, place the waste in your pack or your dog's pack.

When you get back to the trailhead, throw it in the trash. All other hikers will appreciate your actions.

"Nothing is more comical than the look on the face of a person at the upper end of a dog leash, pretending not to know what is going on at the lower."

—*E.B. White* (Essays of E.B. White, *Harper and Row, 1977*)

Whether traveling uphill or down, bicycles have the right of way on trails. Often mountain bikers will warn of their approach with a bike bell. Since this mode of travel can be quite swift, especially on those downhill runs, their approach can be startling to you and your pet. Keep this in mind when starting a trail system, and be on the lookout for mountain bikes.

Step to the downhill side of the trail when encountering horses. Horses have the right of way on trails. Horses consider dogs predators, and so many horses are not comfortable with dogs. Likewise, many dogs are unfamiliar with horses and their sheer size may make dogs uneasy. If you see a horse and rider, immediately take firm control of your dog. Position yourself and your pet on the downhill side of the trail and move off the trail to the side, in clear view of the horse. Keep your dog quiet and in calm control while the horse and rider pass.

Do not assume all other dogs are friendly. It is a fact of life that not all dogs enjoy the company of other dogs. If you are approaching someone with a dog, begin a line of communication by saying, "My dog is friendly, is yours?" This will allow you both to assess the situation before your pets interact with each other. Often we assume that when someone has brought their dog to a public place, the dog must be friendly, but this is not always the case.

Camp away from trails and other visitors. Solitude and privacy are an important part of many hikers' experience. Give others their space to enjoy the outdoors, whether having lunch or camping.

Avoid disturbing wildlife. Having the opportunity to view wildlife can be a truly rewarding experience. The goal is to view the animals without disturbing them. View from a distance, keep your dog quiet and under control, and enjoy the experience.

Let nature's sounds prevail. Avoid loud voices and noises. Part of the wonder of the wild outdoors is the host of different sounds that can be

This horned lizard calls the desert home. (Photo by Ryan Hewitt)

heard. The wind whistling through the pines, the chirping of the birds in the morning; these sounds add to our experience and to others'. Keep human and dog voices low and to a minimum to avoid bothering other people or wild animals in the vicinity.

Permits and Regulations

Over 85 percent of Nevada is publicly owned and managed by state or federal agencies. This is good news for us outdoorsy people with dogs because as long as we abide by the regulations, there is a lot of land to explore.

Aside from having fun, it is important to learn the regulations before you set out on your adventure. All of the hikes in this book are on federal- or state-owned land. Each land manager has different rules and regulations, so make sure you are familiar with the regulations for the area you are visiting.

The regulations outlined below cover the trails presented in this book. The list includes regulations concerning hiking, camping, dogs, and other specific rules that may be applicable. If your interests lead you beyond the trails discussed in this book, please call the land manager and request more information.

Red Rock Canyon National Conservation Area

The U.S. Bureau of Land Management (BLM) manages Red Rock Canyon National Conservation Area (NCA) as well as the majority of unincorporated land around Las Vegas. Since Red Rock is a conservation area, the permits and regulations are more restrictive compared to the remainder of the land managed by the BLM. More information can be obtained by contacting the Red Rock Canyon Visitor Center at (702) 515-5350, or the BLM Las Vegas District Office at (702) 515-5000.

Hiking

Carry out all trash. Hikers should stay on established trails. Cutting across switchbacks damages soils and plants, and severely damages the trail.

Camping

Carry out all trash or properly dispose of it in trash receptacles. Backcountry camping is allowed within Red Rock Canyon NCA above 5000 feet. A permit is required and can be obtained by calling (702) 515-5050. Ground fires are prohibited. Camping stoves are permitted.

Dogs

Pets must be leashed to minimize conflicts with other people, other pets, and native wildlife. This includes at the campground and at other developed facilities such as the visitor center, Willow Springs Picnic Area and Red Rock Overlook. Pets may not be left unattended. Pet owners are

Wild burros are frequently seen at Red Rock Canyon NCA.

required to clean up pet waste (baggies for waste disposal are available in the campground and at the Red Rock Canyon Scenic Drive fee station).

In the campground, pets must be leashed at all times. Pet owners are reminded that temperatures in summertime can reach above 110°F; leaving a pet in a vehicle can endanger its life.

Other Regulations

The burros at Red Rock Canyon NCA are not domesticated, and can be dangerous. Do not feed or pet the burros. Feeding burros encourages these animals to congregate on roadways, where many have been killed or injured by vehicles. To observe these animals safely, pick a safe place to stop, pull completely off the roadway, and observe the burros from a distance. Staying in your car is the safest way to photograph and observe the burros.

Red Rock Canyon NCA is a day-use area with the exception of the developed campground.

The hours of the Red Rock Canyon Scenic Drive are as follows:

- November 1 through February 28/29, 6:00 AM–5:00 PM
- March 1 through March 31, 6:00 AM–7:00 PM
- April 1 through September 30, 6:00 AM–8:00 PM
- October 1 through October 31, 6:00 AM–7:00 PM

The Red Rock Overlook on Nevada Highway 159 (West Charleston Boulevard) is open for one additional hour.

The hours of the visitor center are 8:00 AM–4:30 PM

The following activities require permits in the Red Rock Canyon NCA: backcountry use; collecting of rocks, historical, or natural objects; commercial use; filming; specified rock climbing routes; special events; and weddings.

Bureau of Land Management (BLM)

These regulations apply on BLM land outside of the Red Rock Canyon National Conservation Area:

Hiking

Casual use hiking is permitted on roads, trails, and dry washes outside Areas of Critical Environmental Concern.

Camping

Camping is allowed virtually anywhere outside the Las Vegas Valley unless otherwise noted. There is one developed campground at Red Rock

Canyon NCA, and many primitive camping opportunities. Camping in any one location is limited to fourteen days. Primitive campsites must be located at least 200 feet from roads and water sources. Grey water must be dumped at least 200 feet from any water source. Dumping sewage on public land is illegal. Open campfires are usually not allowed during the summer months due to extreme fire danger. When possible, build fires in existing fire pits.

Dogs
Keep your dog under control. Avoid all wildlife and sensitive plants.

Other Regulations
Federal laws protect all cultural resources over fifty years old, including but not limited to buildings, structures, and trash scatterings containing bottles and cans. It is illegal to disturb historic sites or collect artifacts.

Federal laws protect prehistoric cultural sites, including but not limited to remains of Indian encampments, roasting pits, petroglyphs, and pictographs. It is illegal to disturb these sites or collect artifacts.

United States Forest Service (USFS)
The USFS manages the Spring Mountains National Recreation Area (commonly known as the Mount Charleston area). Since the area has the special designation of Recreation Area, it is managed more strictly than other Forest Service areas. More information can be obtained by contacting the United States Forest Service, Spring Mountains National Recreation Area at (702) 515-5400, or (in emergencies) (702) 872-5306.

Hiking
Stay on the trail. Short-cutting switchbacks causes erosion and destroys the existing trail. Pack out what you pack in. Hikers, mountain bikers, and horse riders share certain trails. Visitors with livestock have the right of way. Be courteous and allow them to pass.

Treat all drinking water by boiling, using water purifiers, or with iodine tablets.

Camping
Take out of the forest what you bring in. Throw garbage and litter in containers provided for this purpose, or take it with you. Fees must be paid before using the site.

Swimming is a cooling respite from the desert heat.

Help protect the vegetation by parking only in paved or marked parking areas.

Do not carve, chop, cut, or damage any trees.

Build fires only in the fire rings or grills. Be sure to extinguish your fire completely before leaving. Ground fires are not permitted in Cathedral Rock Picnic Area.

Do not make unreasonably loud noise that would cause harm or annoyance to other visitors.

Dogs

When hiking, pets must be leashed at all times. Pets must be leashed at all times in the campgrounds and picnic areas.

National Park Service (NPS)

The NPS manages the Lake Mead National Recreation Area. More information concerning regulations at Lake Mead can be obtained by contacting the National Park Service, Alan Bible Visitor Center at (702) 293-8990 and (702) 293-8997.

Hiking

Stay on the designated trails. Many desert soils are fragile and take a long time to recover if disturbed. Rock hounding and collecting plants or animals are prohibited.

Camping

There are four campgrounds that offer restrooms, running water, dump stations, grills, picnic tables, and shade: Boulder Basin, Lake Mojave, Overton Arm, and East Lake Mead. Backcountry camping is also permitted. Numerous areas can be reached by boat, car, backpacking, or horseback. Primitive camping, accessible by boat along the shoreline, is permitted anywhere outside of developed areas except where "No Camping" signs are posted.

Camping is limited to a total of ninety days within any consecutive twelve-month period. Unless otherwise specified, camping is limited to fifteen days per visit at a specific backcountry area. After fifteen days, campers must either move to another backcountry area or developed campground, or leave the park.

When camping in the backcountry, always tell a friend or relative where you are going and when you plan to return. Include a description of your vehicle and your group.

Do not leave fires unattended. Only driftwood collected from below the high-water line may be used in campfires. Firewood may also be purchased at concession stores. Ground fires are permitted only in metal fire rings provided in some of the sites.

Dogs

Pets must be kept at all times on a leash not to exceed six feet in length, and should not be left unattended. (Please note that this includes in the water at the lake or the river.)

Never leave your pet in a closed vehicle. Temperatures can soar to 130°F (54°C) in minutes. Your pet can quickly die of heat stroke in those conditions.

Other Regulations

Please do not feed the wildlife. Animals can become dependent on handouts of food and lose their fear of humans. This is dangerous for the wildlife and you. All plants, animals, and natural features are protected in national parks.

Gypsum soils, often marked by light-colored barren areas, are an ideal habitat for the endangered bear paw poppy and the sunray, one of the most impressive members of the sunflower family. Walk gently here.

Desert springs support a unique community of plants and animals. These springs are often the only source of water for many miles. Be careful not to contaminate them with trash and other human waste.

You lookin' at me?

Please do not touch or disturb any petroglyphs (ancient etchings on rock walls) or archeological sites. If you see anyone defacing a petroglyph or damaging an archaeological site, please report it to a National Park Service ranger.

United States Fish and Wildlife Service (USFWS)

The USFWS manages the Desert National Wildlife Range. More information concerning regulations here can be obtained by contacting the Desert National Wildlife Range at (702) 879-6110. Note: If calling from Las Vegas, you must dial the area code.

Hiking

Vehicles are only permitted on designated roads and all vehicles must be licensed as required by state law. Carry out all you bring in. Do not damage or remove historical or archaeological artifacts. Collection or disturbance of any plant or animal is a violation of federal law.

Camping

Permitted year-round but limited to fourteen consecutive days. No camping within 0.25 mile of water developments or springs. Campfires are permitted, but you need to bring in your own wood. Pack out all waste.

Dogs

All pets must be leashed at all times.

Other Regulations

No carrying or possession of firearms is allowed. The western half of the wildlife range is used by the Nellis Air Force Base as a test and training range. There is no public access to this area.

Nevada State Parks

Valley of Fire is a Nevada State Park. More information concerning rules and regulations in the Valley of Fire can be obtained by contacting the Valley of Fire Visitor Center at (702) 397-2088. Note: If calling from Las Vegas, you must dial the area code.

Hiking

Please stay on designated trails. Be careful with your litter. Use the trash containers provided.

Camping

Camp only in designated campground sites. Fires are permitted only in designated grills and fireplaces.

Dogs

Pets are welcome, but they must be kept on a leash not more than six feet in length. They are not allowed in the visitor center.

Other Regulations

Drive your vehicle only on approved routes of travel and park only in designated places along the roadside shoulders. Motor vehicles are not allowed on trails.

State law protects all plants, animals, and rock and mineral materials in the park. Please do not remove or disturb any rocks, petrified wood, or other natural objects. State and federal laws protect all artifacts and other signs of Indian civilization.

Check at the visitor center for information regarding professional photography in Nevada State Parks. Permits are required.

Go Lightly on the Land

As the population of Las Vegas grows, so does the number of users to our natural areas. We all need to remember that although the desert appears harsh and resilient, it is an extremely fragile environment. Studies have shown that some types of desert soil can take over 200 years to recover from being walked or driven on once. For example, wagon trail tracks across Death Valley are still visible today. Understanding the desert and what areas are sensitive to disturbance is important. Our wild places can be impacted from physical damage such as abrasion, compaction, erosion of the soils, damage to the flora, disturbance of animal life and habitat, and pollution of land and water.

In order to preserve the natural areas that we visit, it is important to apply the guidelines set out by Leave No Trace. Leave No Trace is a national nonprofit organization that strives to educate recreational users about the impact of their actions and how they can reduce such impacts. Resource users have accepted the ideals set by the Leave No Trace program across the country as the best set of ethics to follow. To find more information on this organization and its goals, look online at *www.lnt.org*.

There are seven principles of Leave No Trace that should be considered when hiking with your dog.

1. Plan Ahead and Prepare.

Know the regulations and special concerns for the area you'll visit. Prepare for extreme weather, hazards, and emergencies. Schedule your trip to avoid times of high use. Visit in small groups. Split larger parties into groups of four to six. Repackage food to minimize waste. Use

Camy spins in circles after her booties are put on.

a map and compass to eliminate the use of marking paint, rock cairns, or flagging.

2. Travel and Camp on Durable Surfaces.

Durable surfaces include established trails and campsites, rock, gravel, dry grasses, or snow. Protect riparian areas by camping at least 200 feet from lakes and streams. Good campsites are found, not made. Altering a site is not necessary.

In popular areas:

- Concentrate use on existing trails and campsites.
- Walk single file in the middle of the trail, even when it is wet or muddy.
- Keep campsites small. Focus activity in areas where vegetation is absent.

In pristine areas:

- Disperse use to prevent the creation of campsites and trails.
- Avoid places where impacts are just beginning.

3. Dispose of Waste Properly.

Pack it in, pack it out. Inspect your campsite and rest areas for trash or spilled foods. Pack out all trash, leftover food, and litter. Deposit solid human waste in cat holes dug six to eight inches deep at least 200 feet from water, camp, and trails. Cover and disguise the cat hole when finished. Pack out toilet paper and hygiene products. To wash yourself or your dishes, carry water 200 feet away from streams or lakes and use small amounts of biodegradable soap. Scatter strained dishwater.

4. Leave What You Find.

Preserve the past: Examine, but do not touch, cultural or historic structures and artifacts. Leave rocks, plants, and other natural objects as you find them. Avoid introducing or transporting non-native species. Do not build structures or furniture, or dig trenches.

5. Minimize Campfire Impacts.

Campfires can cause lasting impacts to the backcountry. Use a lightweight stove for cooking and enjoy a candle lantern for light. Where fires are permitted, use established fire rings, fire pans, or mound fires. Keep fires small. Use only sticks from the ground that can be broken by hand. Burn all wood and coals to ash, put out campfires completely, then scatter cool ashes.

6. Respect Wildlife.

Observe wildlife from a distance. Do not follow or approach wildlife. Never feed animals. Feeding wildlife damages their health, alters natural behaviors, and exposes them to predators and other dangers. Protect wildlife and your food by storing rations and trash securely. Control pets at all times, or leave them at home. Avoid wildlife during sensitive times—when they are mating, nesting, raising young, and during winter.

7. Be Considerate of Other Visitors.

Respect other visitors and protect the quality of their experience. Be courteous. Yield to other users on the trail. Step to the downhill side of the trail when encountering pack stock. Take breaks and camp away from trails and other visitors. Let nature's sound prevail. Avoid loud voices and noises.

Camp Care: Cleanup

The desert is an extremely fragile environment. Disturbances we create may take as long as 200 years to heal. For this reason, it is extremely important to use caution when selecting a campsite, and to leave the campsite in better shape than when you found it. When selecting a campsite, keep in mind the Leave No Trace principles and try to camp on a durable surface. When taking down your camp, remember to pack out everything you packed in.

Aside from packing out all of your trash, two common camp hygiene problems are cleaning yourself and your cooking pots. The solutions are similar for both. Do not wash your dishes or yourself directly in water sources. Use as little water as possible and scatter the gray water at least 200 feet from any body of water. When you have to use soap, use one that is biodegradable. When doing your dishes, if you have food left over that you or your dog won't eat, it is best to pack it out. It is also a good idea to strain your dishwater through a piece of cheesecloth or an old shirt, and pack out the bits and pieces in a sealable plastic bag. When washing your body, apply a small drop of biodegradable soap and a little bit of water. Scrub away and then wipe off most of the soap with a towel or piece of clothing. Finally, rinse with water.

Once you have cleaned your site, make a note of where you stayed on your map. Next time you hike through the area, check in on your old campsite and make sure it is in good shape.

Gear for You and Your Dog

Dogs, just like humans, need good hiking gear. There are a host of different brands, levels of sophistication, and price differences for every outdoor product available. The general rule of thumb is to find what works for you and to buy the best you can afford.

Listed below are suggestions for wearable gear for you and your dog:

The shoes. Desert hiking is a bit different from hiking in other areas. A high-grade Gore-Tex or leather may be perfect in the winter but may cook your feet in the summer. Many brands are now producing summer-weight boots with mesh sides for cooling. The longer the hike, the more substantial and supportive the boot typically should be. A short 2-mile hike across the open desert could be completed with a pair of tennis shoes with good tread, but a 10-mile hike up a wash will feel like a 20-mile hike if you're not outfitted with a stiffer, sturdier boot. The shoe obviously needs to fit well, and different brands fit different people better than others. When your shoe is tied, your foot should not slide back and forth, even when you are standing on angled terrain. Shops that specialize in outdoor activities have staff that can assist with your shoe purchase; typically, such shops have an angled rock surface to check for slippage. Socks are really a personal preference; some people prefer thick socks and others thin, but overall try a pair of high-grade hiking socks and feel the difference.

Shoes for our dogs are sometimes important too. We usually think of snow when we think of dog booties, but they can and should be used in the desert as well. The desert has a lot of rocks; some, like sandstone, have the texture of sandpaper; others, like volcanic rock, are sharp. The desert also has cacti that can puncture the skin. Dog booties can help protect your dog's paw pads against these sharp surfaces. As your pet hikes more and more on rough terrain, the pads will toughen and strengthen. It is an advantage to have boots along in case the terrain is particularly rough or a paw becomes injured.

The backpack. Whether for human or canine, a backpack should not be more than 20 percent of the carrier's weight. For instance, a person who weighs 150 pounds should carry a backpack that weighs 30 pounds or less, while a dog that weighs 80 pounds should carry 16 pounds or less. This includes the weight of the pack, not just contents! When selecting a pack, explain your needs to a specialist in an outdoor equipment store. They will help determine which pack fits properly and the appropriate size for your needs. There are a variety of dog packs as well, ranging in quality and design. When filling your dog's pack, remember to balance

Gahby models her dog pack.

the contents evenly. This will help avoid injuries and allow the pack to sit balanced on the dog's back.

Water bottles. When you live in the desert, water is a definite necessity. The low relative humidity makes it easy to become dehydrated, especially during hot weather. Keeping hydrated is essential for our dogs as well as for us. There are a variety of different ways to carry water, but the hydration bladder system is probably the most innovative. These systems store water in a plastic collapsible bladder that fits in a backpack or waist pack. The water is delivered to the wearer via a tube with a valve at the end. This system is very easy to use and enables the wearer to get water without stopping, taking off their pack, and getting out a water bottle.

For wetter, lusher areas of the country, carrying a water purifier is second nature for all long hiking trips. Unfortunately, water sources in the desert are seasonal and unpredictable. It is recommended never to rely on water being available; instead, carry your own water. The exception to this is of course Lake Mead. Another alternative is to contact the land manager of the area and get their insight as to whether a water source is available or not. If you are absolutely certain that a water source will be available, bring your purifier. Even the clearest, purest-looking water can contain parasites and intestinal bacteria such as *E. coli*. These organisms can cause water-borne illnesses, primarily diarrhea and dysentery. More robust pathogens such as *Giardia* are very difficult to recover from. An ounce of prevention—i.e., the time and effort to purify your drinking water—is definitely worth it.

Some people argue that it is healthier to drink large quantities of water over several breaks, rather than taking a sip here and there. Take this into consideration and remember to take longer water breaks on occasion. Another important point in hydration is the replacement of electrolytes. The body can actually lose so many electrolytes that it cannot process water properly. You can still become dehydrated even if you are drinking a lot of water! Bringing along an electrolyte replacement drink (sports drinks) goes a long way in the desert environment. Powdered versions of the drinks can be mixed with water bottles and bladders, or a separate bottle can be carried. For some, these drinks are strong tasting and can be unpleasant. If you fall into this category, dilute the mixture to reduce the concentration.

Just as humans do, our canine companions need water on a regular basis when hiking in the desert. There are a variety of collapsible dog bowls on the market today that are easy to transport. Also available is a uniquely designed water bottle with a cone bowl attached to the top. When you squeeze the bottle, the bowl fills up and your dog can drink out of it. Another option is to teach your dog to drink from a water stream sent their way from your bladder bag or water bottle. Dogs will try to get to the water tube when they are thirsty. If you go about providing water for your dog this way, just make sure your dog is getting enough. Much of the water may miss the dog's mouth and end up on the ground.

Clothes. There are basic guidelines for clothes to wear when desert hiking: light-colored, loose-fitting, and fully covering the skin. Dark colors absorb the heat and make you hotter. For this reason, black or dark blue are colors you should not wear in the hot summer months, but they may be suitable in the winter. During the rest of the year, stick with light colors, such as tan or white, which reflect the sun's rays. Loose-fitting clothes tend to be more cooling. The air circulates under the clothing, allowing your skin to cool. Finally, select clothes that completely cover your skin. This includes wearing a hat with a wide brim so your face, ears, and neck are shaded. Also, a long-sleeved loose shirt will protect your arms. Pants protect your legs from the sun as well as rocks and cacti.

You may also want to consider wearing performance-designed clothing materials instead of cotton. Cotton is a poor choice when hiking because it retains moisture. The new fabrics and clothes that are available are designed with exercising in mind. Some are very lightweight, water-wicking, and have an SPF rating. There are several manufacturers out there and, although you may raise an eye at some of the prices, they really are worth the investment. With more competition in the past few years, there are some lower-priced alternatives as well. If you only hike on the weekends, you may need only one sun-protection shirt and pant. Check with your local sporting good stores or shop online for this type of clothing.

Once you have a pack, what should you put in it? The Ten Essentials cover the necessities:

Ten Essentials: A Systems Approach
1. Navigation (map and compass)
2. Sun protection (sunglasses and sunscreen)
3. Insulation (extra clothing)
4. Illumination (headlamp or flashlight)
5. First-aid supplies
6. Fire (firestarter and matches/lighter)
7. Repair kit and tools (including knife)
8. Nutrition (extra food)
9. Hydration (extra water)
10. Emergency shelter

Canine Ten Essentials
You should also have the ten essentials for your dog:

1. **Obedience training.** Before you set foot on a trail, make sure your dog is trained and can be trusted to behave when faced with other hikers, other dogs, wildlife, and an assortment of strange scents and sights in the backcountry.
2. **Doggy backpack.** Lets the dog carry its own gear.
3. **Basic first-aid kit** (details listed later in this chapter).
4. **Dog food and trail treats.** You should take more food than your dog normally consumes since it will be burning more calories than normal, and if you do end up having to spend an extra night out there, you need to keep the pup fed, too. Trail treats serve the same

purpose for the dog as they do for you—quick energy and a pick-me-up during a strenuous day of hiking.

5. **Water and water bowl.** Don't count on there being water along the trail for the dog. Pack enough extra water to meet all your dog's drinking needs.

6. **Leash and collar, or harness.** Even if your dog is absolutely trained to voice command and stays at heel without a leash, sometimes leashes are required by law or just by common courtesy, so you should have one handy at all times.

7. **Insect repellent.** Be aware that some animals, and some people, have strong negative reactions to DEET-based repellents. So, before leaving home, dab a little DEET-based repellent on a patch of your dog's fur to see if it reacts to it. Look for signs of drowsiness, lethargy, and/or nausea. Restrict repellent applications to those places the dog can't lick—the back of the neck and around the ears (staying well clear of the ears and inner ears) are the most logical places mosquitoes will be looking for exposed skin to bite.

8. **ID tags and picture identification.** Your dog should always wear ID tags, and I'd heartily recommend microchipping it as well. To do this, a vet injects a tiny encoded microchip under the skin between a dog's shoulders. If your dog ever gets lost and is picked up by animal control, or is taken to a vet's office, a quick pass over the dog's back with a hand scanner will reveal the chip, and allow the staff at that shelter or hospital to identify your dog and notify you. Microchipping is so prevalent that virtually every veterinarian and animal shelter automatically scans every unknown dog they come in contact with to check for chips. The picture identification should go in your pack. If your dog gets lost, you can use the picture to make flyers and handbills to post in the surrounding communities.

9. **Dog booties.** These can be used to protect the dog's feet from rough ground or harsh vegetation. They are also great at keeping bandages secure if the dog damages its pads.

10. **Compact roll of plastic bags and trowel.** You'll need the bags to clean up after your dog on popular trails. When conditions warrant, you can use the trowel to take care of your dog's waste. Just pretend you are a cat—dig a small hole several inches deep in the forest duff, deposit the dog waste, and fill in the hole.

Health and Fitness Concerns for Your Dog

Just as people come in a variety of different physical fitness levels, so do dogs. The condition of your dog must be taken into account when you choose your level of activity. Young dogs and older dogs are more susceptible to difficult terrain and temperature extremes. If you are unsure of your pet's capabilities, see a veterinarian for a health evaluation prior to hiking. Also, take it slow and see how your pet does in a variety of situations before hitting the difficult hikes. Starting a daily exercise routine is helpful for both dog and human to develop the muscles and stamina that will be used on the trails.

A young dog will actually need to be taught, or to teach itself through experience, how to rock scramble. The first few times, there may be some unsure footing and possible falls. Some dogs are more adapted to hiking

Lexus likes drinking directly from water bottles.

than other dogs as well. Be realistic about your dog's capabilities. Also, remember that dogs are creatures that love the outdoors; with practice, most dogs can have a rewarding outdoor experience.

In a desert environment, issues like dehydration and overheating must be dealt with for our pets as well as ourselves. Any of the short-snouted breeds like the English bulldog or Boston terrier are more susceptible to overheating in high temperatures. The shorter snout does not enable the dog to cool itself as easily as other dog breeds. For this reason, these dogs should be watched carefully when exercising.

Another thing to consider is your dog's coat. Coats that are dark in color or very thick will cause your dog to get hot quickly when the sun is shining high. Dogs that have long coats are also more susceptible to getting twigs, grass seeds, and burrs caught in their fur. If you hike with your dog frequently, consider trimming its coat. On the flip side, dogs with very short coats can get sunburned or cold. If your dog fits into this category, consider a doggie sweater.

Footpad durability depends on an individual dog's skin toughness and thickness, and is somewhat breed-dependent as well. A slow introduction to harder substrates helps to toughen up footpads to get ready for hiking. Dogs' pads come in a variety of thicknesses and durability. Some dogs can hike miles on a scrambling route without any problems. Others may walk 0.25 mile and have worn their pads. This is where dog booties come in. You may typically think of dog booties for snow environments, but they are indispensable in desert environments. The terrain here is harsh. There are areas of very sharp rocks, cacti with spines and, due to the hot weather, *very* hot substrates. Sandstone can act like sandpaper on paws and nails, and rocky or gravelly terrain can be abrasive as well. If the majority of a dog's activity is on soft substrates, the rougher trail environments can be too harsh for their paws. Their footpads and nails can become worn and begin to bleed. Use flour or cornmeal to stop the bleeding, and put a dog bootie on that foot. Dog booties can be purchased at pet stores and outdoor sporting good stores. Homemade booties using leather are a great alternative to those commercially available.

Canine First Aid

Hiking in the desert comes with some naturally occurring dangers and issues that need to be addressed: overheating (hyperthermia) and heat stroke, hypothermia, foot pad and nail injuries, sore muscles, poisonous plants, and potentially dangerous wildlife. Education and prevention are key in avoiding or handling a first-aid concern that arises. Remember that your pet can't tell you if it is feeling ill, sore, or hurt, so watch your pet carefully for signs of suffering.

Preventative health. Regular veterinarian examinations and vaccinations are crucial for your pet's health and should be considered as preventative first aid. Discuss with the veterinarian your desire to begin hiking with your pet. The veterinarian may want to discuss with you specific issues relating to your pet's health before you embark into the wilderness. Exercise is also imperative. Walk your dog regularly so it stays fit.

Worn pads and nails. The most likely first-aid situation you will face will be worn pads and nails on your pet. Part of the fun of hiking in this area is its diverse terrain and the occasional rock scrambling. Rock surfaces can be as harsh as a file on paws and nails. For hiking, a dog's nails should be clipped to a medium length but not short. Nails that are too short can wear down easily on rock surfaces such as sandstone. Sandstone feels like fine sandpaper, so it really isn't surprising how quickly it can wear down dog nails and pads. Pad durability on the trail is dependent on the toughness and thickness of the pad surface. Some breeds tend to have thinner, more sensitive pads. You can help your dog develop tougher, thicker pads by walking it regularly on harder substrates such as gravel or pavement. If your pet has a worn pad or nail, apply flour or cornstarch to stop the bleeding. Once the bleeding has ceased, protect the site from farther injury or trauma. Keep a pair of dog booties in your pack in case an injury occurs. They protect the sensitive area for the remainder of the hike.

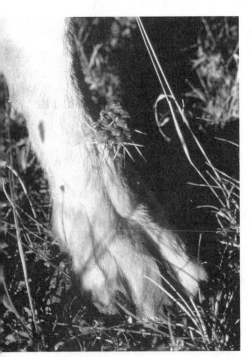

Cacti are a common hazard in desert hiking.

Cacti. You might not think of

tweezers as a prime component of a first-aid kit, but here in the Mojave Desert they are a necessity. This area has a variety of cacti with a host of different types of spines. Some are very fine and will break off easily. Others have spines that will go through the bottom of a hiking boot. You will pat yourself on the back for your foresight and good thinking if you are faced with the unfortunate situation of being stuck by a cactus and you have a pair of tweezers handy. Although cacti do on occasion stick dogs, this happens surprisingly less often than you might think. Dogs seem to be able to maneuver their way among cacti without much contact. A dog's behavior will usually let you know when it has been stuck, such as lifting a paw or licking an area. In some cases, removal of the spine is straightforward. In others, sedation may be necessary. If unsure whether you can remove the spine, or if you think the spine may break off, take your pet to a veterinarian for treatment. After removal, check the injury in the days following to ensure the site has not become infected.

Dehydration, hyperthermia, and heat stroke. Dogs do not sweat as humans do; they rely on rapid breathing—panting—to cool their bodies. When the air temperature nears a dog's body temperature (101°F), this cooling method is not efficient, rendering the animal susceptible to heat-related illnesses. Dogs can also become dehydrated when they do not receive enough water to drink. Signs of dehydration are increased heart rate and dry gums. Hyperthermia is an elevation in body temperature that occurs from exposure to very hot environments. Extreme hyperthermia can lead to heat stroke, which happens as a dog's organ systems begin to malfunction due to overheating. Signs of heat stroke are rapid heartbeat, panting, excessive salivation, and, in more extreme situations, shock, coma, and respiratory arrest. Heat-related illnesses are very serious and it is imperative to seek veterinarian advice as soon as possible. Immediate care includes cooling of the dog with fans, or wetting it with water. Wetting the dog's pads is a quick method for cooling down the animal. Discontinue all cooling treatment once the dog has cooled to normal temperatures. Continuing can chill the dog and cause hypothermia. Avoiding dehydration is the best prevention for any of these heat-related illnesses. To keep hydrated, a dog needs to drink water on a regular basis. On a hot day, it wouldn't be uncommon to stop for water every 20–30 minutes. When hiking, stop frequently and offer your dog water. On hotter days, make sure your friend has even more water than usual. Note: a dog can vomit if given water that is too cold, so keep the water cool but not ice cold.

Even seasoned hikers like Mollie sometimes injure their paws.

Hypothermia. Hypothermia occurs when exposure to extreme cold chills the whole body. Water, snow, and ice can cool a dog quickly and may cause hypothermia. Dogs with low body fat are more susceptible to the cold and should be watched carefully when swimming or in cold environments. Early signs of hypothermia include extreme shivering, followed by lethargy and finally collapse. Wrap the dog in a blanket or coat and seek veterinarian assistance.

Stomach turning, or torsion. Larger-breed dogs with deep chests such as Labradors, boxers, Saint Bernards, and standard poodles are all susceptible to the condition of stomach turning. This condition is seen in bigger dogs that tend to eat and drink large amounts in one sitting. When the stomach is full and extended, it can twist in a way that cuts off its blood flow. This condition is extremely serious and can cause death quickly. Signs of torsion include an enlarged, bloated abdomen, rapid breathing, salivating with pale gums, and in some cases collapsing. Luckily, this condition, though extremely serious, is easily avoided. When on the trail, do not allow the dog to drink large amounts of water at one time. Have the dog drink, take a break, then drink again. More frequent, smaller amounts of water are key to keeping your dog optimally hydrated throughout the hike.

Sore muscles. It happens to all of us, whether canine or human. You head out on the trail and your day ends up being harder than you thought it would be. If your dog is having a hard time with sore muscles or arthritis, speak to your veterinarian about using aspirin for pain relief. Your vet will be able to assess whether this is appropriate for your dog, and what dosages should be used. Never give a dog ibuprofen or acetaminophen; these drugs can be toxic to dogs and may cause organ damage.

Emergency care. After a serious injury, it is essential to assess the extent of the injury. Since the injury could be quite extensive and painful to the dog, it is important to take the precautionary measure of muzzling the dog. Use a traditional muzzle or bandage material from the first-aid kit. Assess the situation; immobilize the area if there is a break, and then transport the dog to a veterinarian.

Puncture wound. For a puncture wound, apply slight pressure until bleeding has ceased. Then clean the area with an iodine-based antiseptic or hydrogen peroxide followed by the application of a triple-antibiotic ointment. Bandage the area and have the dog examined by a veterinarian.

Head trauma. After a head trauma it is essential to assess the severity of the situation. Using a penlight, look at both of the dog's eyes and examine the pupils. Using the chart below, determine the severity and extent of the injury and seek veterinarian attention accordingly.

Severity	Pupil Size (Pupil reaction when light is applied)	Reactivity	Prognosis
Least Severe	Normal	Normal	Good
	Bilateral constriction	Poor to nonresponsive	Guarded
	One sided dilation	Poor to nonresponsive	Guarded-poor
	Normal size	Nonresponsive	Guarded-poor
Most Severe	Both sides dilated	Poor to nonresponsive	Poor

Snake bite. A common question from hikers in this area is, "What happens if my dog or I get bitten by a rattlesnake?" First of all, the rattlesnake is not a demon creature lurking around, waiting to attack you or your dog.

Like any other species, rattlesnakes spend their time trying to find food, shelter, and, if they are lucky, a mate. Consider an encounter between you, your dog, and a snake from the snake's perspective: You are too big to be food and you are not a potential mate. To the snake you are simply a predator, something that may do it harm. Luckily, the rattlesnake is mostly a nocturnal creature (it sleeps during the day and is awake at night) and, therefore, encounters with rattlesnakes are rare. The snake's striking distance is only about one-half its length (or less), so you would need to be in close proximity to be bitten. Another plus is that a large portion of initial, defensive bites are "dry," meaning little or no venom has been injected.

If a snake bites you or your dog, don't panic. Less than 0.1 percent of snakebites to humans (less than one in 1000) are fatal. Whether human or canine, the young and elderly are more susceptible to the effects of the venom. If you are carrying a cell phone, call the local hospital or veterinarian (as appropriate) and give vital information such as age, weight, height, and general health of the bite victim. Tell the health facility your approximate time of arrival.

Do not try to treat the bite yourself; the old method of cutting the bite wound and sucking out the venom is not recommended! Instead, wrap the area with a bandage, firmly but not tightly—about as tight as you would wrap a sprained ankle. The bandage's purpose is to slow down the blood flow but not stop it. Using a tourniquet, which severely restricts or even stops blood flow, can cause serious injury. Continue calmly to your vehicle and to medical help.

Dogs are typically not as affected by rattlesnake bites as are humans, but a bite to a dog's face could cause severe swelling, possibly preventing breathing. For canines and humans alike, a rattlesnake bite is serious and requires immediate professional medical attention.

A Doggy First-Aid Kit

Having a dog first-aid kit is necessary, even if it has only the bare-bones essentials. For a comprehensive canine first-aid kit though, anyone heading into the wild with a canine companion should carry the following essentials:

Instruments
- Scissors/bandage scissors/toenail clippers
- Rectal thermometer (a healthy dog should show a temperature of 101°F when taken rectally)

Cleansers and disinfectants
- 3 % hydrogen peroxide
- Betadine
- Canine eyewash (available at any large pet supply store).

Topical antibiotics and ointments (nonprescription)
- Calamine lotion
- Triple antibiotic ointment (Bacitracin, Neomycin, or Polymyxin)
- Baking soda (for bee stings)
- Vaseline
- Stop-bleeding powder

Medications
- Enteric-coated aspirin or Bufferin
- Imodium-AD
- Pepto-Bismol

Dressings and bandages
- Gauze pads (4 inches square), or gauze roll
- Nonstick pads
- Adhesive tape (1-inch and 2-inch rolls)

Miscellaneous
- Muzzle
- Dog boots
- Any prescription medication your dog needs

For extended trips

Consult your vet about any other prescription medications that may be needed in emergency situations, including:
- Oral antibiotics
- Eye/ear medications
- Emetics (to induce vomiting)
- Pain medications and anti-inflammatories
- Suturing materials for large open wounds

Wildlife

At first glance, many newcomers think, "What kind of wildlife could possibly exist here except for rattlesnakes?" There are in fact many species that have adapted to the harsh conditions of the Mojave Desert. In Red Rock Canyon alone, there are over forty-five species of mammals. Cool canyons and perennial water sources provide these animals with ways to escape the heat and aridity.

There are two important factors when considering our local wildlife. First of all, as stewards of the land we need to ensure the safety of the wildlife. We are entering their environment, so we need to respect their space, water sources, and food. We are lucky to have many endemic species here that live nowhere else in the world. We need to ensure that our presence doesn't negatively affect these creatures. Keeping our pets in firm control and staying on designated trails reduces our impact. Second, it is important to be aware of the effects these creatures can have on us. Which species are we most likely to encounter and what should our reaction be? Below are some animals, birds, and insects that live in the desert that you should be aware of. If you take proper precautions, your adventures on the trails will be safe and enjoyable for you and your dog.

Mammals

There are many species of mammals in this area, ranging from the small kangaroo rat to the mountain lion. Regardless of the size or type of animal, do not allow your dog to approach wild animals, whether living or dead. Diseases can be spread to your pet from close contact with an animal, even a deceased one.

Probably one of the more common large mammals is the coyote. The coyote is a common resident in the Southwestern deserts including the Las Vegas area. It is a relative of the dog that communicates through barks and howls. The coyote is an adaptable species that has taken advantage of development in the Las Vegas Valley and can be commonly seen in urban neighborhoods and golf courses. Coyotes, although quite abundant, avoid contact with humans and dogs, commonly fleeing when they notice humans. Never attempt to approach a coyote or allow your dog to approach or chase one.

There are several large wild cats that inhabit our desert. Both the bobcat and the mountain lion (cougar) have been reported in the region. At present, these cats do not exist in large numbers and encounters are unlikely. They are more common in secluded natural areas with sufficient food, water, and some solitude. These creatures typically shy away from human contact.

In mountain lion country, the Nevada Department of Wildlife suggests the following:

- Do not jog or bike in an area known to have mountain lions
- Hike in groups
- Make lots of noise
- Keep children close to you
- Never approach a lion
- Stay calm
- Stop or move slowly away
- Appear as large and loud as possible. Do not bend over.

The goal is to have the mountain lion believe that you are a very large creature and that you are retreating, not fleeing. By running, you will trigger a pursuit. Unlike with a bear, if you are physically attacked by a cougar, fight back. Use whatever is available to you: rocks, water bottles, or a hiking stick. In this region, mountain lions tend to be in remote areas, and rarely are there any confrontations between man and lion.

For people from lusher environments, it may surprise you to know we have mule deer and elk in the area. Although these animals are prey species, they are large and, if confronted directly by a dog, may kick, resulting in death or injury. It is important to keep pets in control and on a leash to eliminate any direct contact with large animals.

The bighorn sheep are shy creatures about the size of a small deer. They can be found in Nevada, Arizona, Utah, California, Texas, and northern Mexico. Their coloring allows them to blend incredibly well into the desert landscape. The bighorn roam in small groups, primarily in rugged terrain. Male bighorn have large horns that can form a full curl by age eight. The female is slightly smaller than the male with smaller, narrower horns that are never more than a half curl. These creatures feed throughout the day, and then move to bedding spots for the night. The bighorn sheep rutting season begins in late June and ends in the middle of December. During this period there is much activity within the herd of bighorn sheep, thus increasing the chance for sightings while hiking. Remember, however, that during this time the males are very driven and bold. Keep a safe distance and do not approach the bighorn. Bighorn sheep consider dogs to be predators, so their presence can be very disturbing to them. For this reason, never allow your dog to approach bighorn sheep. Also, bighorn sheep use many of the watering holes found throughout the desert. If you linger by the water for long periods, you may scare away wildlife.

The sight of a wild horse or burro reminds us nostalgically of the Wild West. Nevada has over half of the nation's total number of wild horses. These creatures are abundant and readily seen in several locations in the region. U.S. Public Law 92-195 protects horses and burros. The law protects these creatures from harassment and assists in their management. Usually in small groups, the horses and burros typically stay with their own kind. The herds tend to keep their distance from humans. Watch your dogs carefully; many dogs are apprehensive and can become frightened when encountering a horse or burro.

Rodents fill an important niche in our Mojave Desert environment. Typically, the only rodent you will see on the trail is the antelope ground squirrel. This squirrel has an endearing demeanor with quick movements and a flicking of its tail. But no matter how cute it is, never approach any rodent in the wild and stay clear of any area showing signs of rodent activity. Hantavirus is a very serious disease in the Southwest deserts, carried by rodents. The virus is transmitted from rodent feces and urine, infecting the human lungs. It can be transmitted via direct contact with the feces or urine, or by contact with dirt contaminated with these materials.

Reptiles

The southern Nevada area is home to a host of snakes, lizards, and the perennial favorite, the desert tortoise. Since reptiles are exothermic (they do not produce their own body heat), they rely on the ambient outdoor temperatures to heat their bodies. The best chance to see desert reptiles is when temperatures are between 65–95°F. When the temperature is below this range, reptiles are sluggish and fairly stationary. When temperatures are higher than this range, reptiles will be hiding in burrows and rocky crevices and under bushes to stay cool.

Many of our resident reptiles are commonly seen, and a real treat to watch. The desert tortoise is one such appealing resident in our desert; to see one is a real delight. The chuckwalla is a large, thick-bodied lizard that has almost comical movements and looks. Many dogs find tortoises and lizards interesting and can harass these reptiles. It is important to protect our native reptiles from the harm dogs can inflict. The desert tortoise is a federally-listed threatened species, and it is a punishable offense to harm or harass them. Harassment can be as simple as blocking their path. If you encounter a tortoise, secure your dog and stand back, allowing the tortoise to go on its way. Tortoises actually move much quicker than you would expect.

Nevada is home to seven different species of venomous reptiles. We have the only venomous lizard in the United States, the Gila monster. Although the Gila monster exists in this area, it is rarely seen. The Gila monster is a large lizard, typically twelve inches or so in length, with a black face and irregular black bands across an orange-to-pink-colored body. Although venomous, they are easily seen and avoided. No confirmed human fatalities have resulted from the bite of this lizard.

In the greater Las Vegas area, there are three venomous snakes: the Mojave Desert sidewinder, the Mojave rattlesnake, and the Southwestern speckled rattlesnake. The Southwestern speckled rattlesnake is the most common of these three. This snake's color is variable and ranges from brown to gray to orange, depending upon the terrain in which it lives. The Mojave Desert sidewinder is small, normally 23 inches long or less, is light in coloring (tan, cream, pink, gray, or sandy) with darker patches on its back of gray, yellow, or tan. Typically, this snake occupies low terrains such as valley bottoms. The Mojave rattlesnake, sometimes called the Mojave green, is a larger snake (up to 4 feet long) with a brown to greenish color and a diamond pattern distinctly outlined in white across its back.

The desert tortoise (federally protected species) is a common sight in the cooler hours. (Photo by Ed Remington)

This snake prefers creosote bush-covered flats and low-angled slopes. Two other venomous snake species live in the edges of our immediate region. The Panamint rattlesnake makes its home from the Spring Mountains to the northwest of Las Vegas. The western diamondback can be found in the extreme southern part of Clark County near Laughlin.

Birds

For birders, the Las Vegas Valley has a host of different bird species; some are year-round residents and others migrate through. Many of the visitor centers have a species list of the birds that have been seen in their area. Rangers often have information about breeding areas, seasonal inhabitants, and good locations to go birding.

Although you may not think of birds as a hazard, little dogs beware! It is not uncommon for the larger birds of prey, such as the red-tailed hawk, to circle small dogs and assess whether these little canines would make a good meal. Putting smaller dogs on leash holds the hawks at bay and keeps our pets safe.

With the movement of West Nile virus into our area, it is important to keep away from any dead birds. Mosquitoes carrying the West Nile virus feed on birds and can move to humans if in close proximity (see "Insects and Spiders," below, for more information).

Insects and Spiders

The world of insects and spiders is an interesting interconnected realm of pollinators, predators, and debris feeders. While outdoors, take time to enjoy and learn about these small yet critical members of our ecosystem. There are many insect field guides that can be used for general identification and information about each insect type. Tarantula hawks, large black wasp-like insects, are common in our natural environment and are stunning to see with their velvety black bodies. And, yes, we have tarantulas in this area. Consider it a treat if you see the black furry spider wandering across the trail. They are fun to watch, but don't worry—they don't want to hurt you. Colorful dragonflies and damselflies inhabit areas near water sources. Perhaps one of the most stunning creatures of the desert is the white-lined sphinx moth. This beautifully marked insect is very large; in fact, it is often mistaken for a hummingbird. It flies from flower to flower, drinking nectar.

Bees are found as well in desert environments. Over the past decade, the Africanized honeybee has moved into our vicinity and become established. The Africanized bee is visually undistinguishable from an ordinary bee but is much more aggressive in protecting its hive. If you encounter a swarm of bees, move out of the area quickly. Dark or bright, intensely-colored clothing evokes a more aggressive behavior from the bees; therefore, wearing light-colored clothing is advantageous. Bees will chase for some distance, up to .25 mile, and are attracted to the carbon dioxide in exhaled breath. Covering the face with clothing can reduce stings in this sensitive area. If you have an allergy to bee stings, it is imperative to carry a bee-sting kit for your pro-

Consider yourself lucky if you see a desert tarantula. (Photo by Ryan Hewitt)

tection, and to talk to your physician before hitting the trails.

You may not think of the desert Southwest as a tick and flea area, but they are here. Although not in high quantities, both ticks and fleas can be found in areas such as Mount Charleston. Bubonic plague has recently been documented in wild foxes in that area. The plague is a bacterial illness transmitted by fleas. All sick or dead animals should be avoided to reduce any potential infection. Pets can be protected with flea collars and topical flea and tick medications, and their owners can wear insect repellent. The plague causes exhaustion, headache, fever, and chills. Although dogs rarely suffer severe illness when exposed to the plague, exposure to humans is serious and life-threatening. If an infection is suspected, see your physician.

The West Nile virus has unfortunately made its way to this region. This virus affects humans, birds, horses, and mosquitoes. West Nile virus is transferred to humans from mosquitoes that feed on infected birds. Mosquitoes can be found near areas of standing water such as stagnant ponds. Protect yourself against the mosquitoes, and thus the virus, by wearing long-sleeved shirts and long pants, and using insect repellent containing DEET. The majority of people (80 percent) who become infected with the virus never show any symptoms. Others show mild flu-like symptoms, and a small percentage become seriously ill.

Weather

In the greater Las Vegas area there are extreme desert conditions including harsh, cold winters and really hot summers. With the range in elevations here, you can literally swim in Lake Mead on the same day you have a snowball fight at Mount Charleston.

The late summer, August and September, is the monsoon or rainy

Maynard plays in the snow at Mount Charleston. (Photo by Scott McNulty)

season. Although we also receive rain in the winter and spring, the monsoons are more predictable. Monsoon rains are short yet heavy storms, commonly resulting in flash floods. Flash floods are the most serious danger you are likely to encounter. They are much more common than a mountain lion attack or a rattlesnake bite. The rain falls so fast and hard that the ground cannot soak up all the water, causing the water to flow downhill rapidly. In particular, dry washes will quickly swell with water. Often a wave of water will barrel down the wash, frequently traveling upwards of twenty-five miles per hour.

One of the most important facts to remember is that it does not have to be raining where you are for you to get stuck in a flash flood. How could that be possible? Rain falling miles away can quickly flow down canyons and washes to meet you downstream. If it begins to rain or you see water flowing down a wash or canyon, get to higher ground. Watch weather reports before venturing out to get an idea of any storm systems in your vicinity.

Although we do have occasional lightning storms, they are not as abundant as the storms seen in other areas like southern Arizona. If you are caught in a lightning storm, here are a few tips to follow:

- Avoid mountain peaks
- Move to lower ground
- Remove metal-framed packs
- Crouch down and have as little of your body as possible touching the ground

Using This Book

This book is a guidebook, an introduction to the trails and what you may find there. Some trails and dirt roads may have seasonal changes due to storm systems, improvements, or closures. Contact the land manager before hiking to get the latest information on road and trail conditions. Phone numbers and website addresses for land managers are given with each trail description.

All distances are given as round trips to give an accurate representation of the amount of effort required to accomplish the hike. Distances were gathered with the use of GPS units. While this is a fairly accurate form of measurement, distances from unit to unit may vary slightly. The elevation range is given so the hiker can determine proper clothing requirements and altitude considerations. The hike difficulty is meant to be representative for the majority of hikers. It may appear under- or over-rated, depending on your physical fitness level. Hiking time is based on an average speed of 1 mile in 30 minutes while taking into account trail conditions. The "Under Foot and Paw" heading is meant to give you an idea of what to expect on the hike and to better determine whether your dog will be suited for this particular hike. We also include information on water availability for the pups. The land managers' regulations and contact information are provided so you know the rules of the area, and where to get more information if needed. When a more detailed map is needed than what is presented in this book, you may want to purchase the USGS map for the area. These maps can be purchased at local map stores or online. If you plan on hiking a lot, a great alternative is a computer mapping program. Before each hike you can print out the maps you will need and take them with you. Mapping programs are available online, at a variety of bookstores, and at outdoor gear shops.

The canine health information provided in this book was written under the supervision of Dr. Daniel Diaz, a licensed veterinarian at the Pebble Maryland Animal Hospital in Las Vegas. For health questions specific to your pet, consult your personal veterinarian.

The information about reptiles was written under the supervision of Alex L. Heindl, Curator of Herpetology, Marjorie Barrick Museum of Natural History at the University of Nevada, Las Vegas. The information provided here is not intended as medical advice. All venomous reptile bites require immediate medical attention from a qualified professional.

For more information on insect- and animal-transmitted diseases such as plague and West Nile virus, contact the Clark County Health District at (702) 385-1291, or *www.cchd.org*.

How the Trails Were Selected

For this book, we looked for great hiking trails for you and your dog. The trails were selected with the following criteria in mind:

1. **Trails with shade.** Depending on the season, the sun and heat can be brutal in the desert. Shade along the trail allows you and your pup to cool down.
2. **Trails with water.** For some dogs, the only important things in life are swimming, tennis balls, and food. Everything else is just a bonus. For these dogs we have included hikes with access to watering holes. Almost half of the hikes in this book have water available at some point in the season for the pooches.
3. **Trails with few people.** Some people flat out don't like dogs on

trails, and some dogs don't like people on trails. Unfortunately, small populations of irresponsible dog owners have caused this resentment, and the rest of us get to deal with the repercussions. Just the same, hiking in unpopulated areas is often much nicer than hiking on a trail with a lot of other people!

4. **Trails within three hours of Las Vegas.** If you drive away from Las Vegas for much more than three hours, you are either going to end up in a different state or in a completely different physical environment. The trails within this book are all within three hours of Las Vegas.

5. **A variety of trail lengths and difficultly levels.** Different people and dogs want different types of hikes—some easy and some hard, some short and some long. This book has trails for everyone.

6. **Only approved trails.** The appropriate land managers have approved the use of all the trails in this book. By hiking on approved trails we are all better stewards of the land. Sensitive plants are avoided. Restoration areas are not disturbed. And in the case of an emergency, search-and-rescue personnel know where to look.

Enjoy the Trails: Get Involved

The first and foremost goal of this book is to provide you and your dog with places to go have fun, where both of you will be safe. Hiking can be a great way for humans and canines alike to improve both their health and state of mind. Getting out in nature can be a calming, centering, and overall health-improving experience. If you enjoy your experiences exploring the Mojave Desert, get involved! By being active in protecting Mojave Desert recreational areas, you can make your voice heard. What is great about an area? What is lacking there? Let recreational land managers know what you think.

Getting involved can mean anything from joining in a half-day cleanup to making an ongoing commitment. Here are some specific ways to get involved:

Keep informed. Stay up-to-date with what each of the state and federal agencies around the Las Vegas region is doing.

Let your voice be heard. Write letters to the region's elected officials and tell them what you think and how you feel.

Volunteer. Volunteer with one of the land management agencies or other organizations around town. The Bureau of Land Management (BLM) and National Park Service (NPS) have great volunteer programs where you can lead hikes, teach environmental education programs, or just stuff envelopes! Additional help is always appreciated and needed. Any skills you have to offer will help.

Support those organizations you believe in. Support local dog organizations including (but not limited to) the Society for the Prevention of Cruelty to Animals (SPCA) and no-kill shelters. The cities of Las Vegas, North Las Vegas, and Henderson all offer dog parks for local dog enthusiasts. Support and care for these areas so they continue to exist.

Another fun way to get yourself and your dog involved in your community is to volunteer with programs that bring dogs into hospitals to visit with patients.

"If you can't decide between a Shepherd, a Setter or a Poodle, get them all. . . . Adopt a mutt."

—*(SPCA slogan)*

A Note About Safety

Safety is an important concern in all outdoor activities. No guidebook can alert you to every hazard or anticipate the limitations of every reader. Therefore, the descriptions of roads, trails, routes, and natural features in this book are not representations that a particular place or excursion will be safe for your party. When you follow any of the routes described in this book, you assume responsibility for your own safety. Under normal conditions, such excursions require the usual attention to traffic, road and trail conditions, weather, terrain, the capabilities of your party, and other factors. Because many of the lands in this book are subject to development and/or change of ownership, conditions may have changed since this book was written that make your use of some of these routes unwise. Always check for current conditions, obey posted private property signs, and avoid confrontations with property owners or managers. Keeping informed on current conditions and exercising common sense are the keys to a safe, enjoyable outing.

The Mountaineers Books

PART 2

The Trails

"Of course what [your dog] most intensely dreams
of is being taken out for walks, and the more
you are able to indulge him the more he will
adore you and the more all the latent beauty of
his nature will come out."

—Henry James (in The Complete Notebooks of
Henry James, Leon Edel and Lyall H. Powers [Eds.],
Oxford University Press, 1988.)

DESERT NATIONAL WILDLIFE RANGE

Here in Nevada we have the largest national wildlife refuge outside of Alaska. This refuge, the Desert National Wildlife Range, established in 1936, encompasses 1.5 million acres of land ranging from desert scrub vegetation communities to pine forests. This remote and isolated area also hosts a variety of wildlife. Several hundred species of birds can be found on the refuge, along with reptiles, bighorn sheep, mule deer, coyotes, foxes, bobcats, and mountain lions (see "Wildlife" in Part I, for safety concerns).

Although the Desert National Wildlife Range is set aside for the protection of all wildlife types, its main objective is maintaining the desert bighorn sheep populations. In 2001, an estimated 700 bighorn sheep were living in the Range. It is not uncommon to see bighorn sheep scaling the hillsides when you are driving to a trailhead or hiking with your dog.

If you and your dog would like to avoid crowds of people when hiking and exploring, this area is a great alternative. In some ways it is similar to the Mount Charleston area. The Range has areas with high elevations up to nearly 10,000 feet, so during the warm weather months, there will be cooler temperatures in parts of the Range. Your dog will enjoy the shade provided on many of the trails, thanks to all the pine trees. Most notable, though, is the lack of people. If either you or your dog does not like encountering other people on the trail, this is the place to go. Frequently, if you stop and sign in at the visitor logbook (please do—portions of the Range's funding comes from visitor use) there will not be anybody else signed in that day. Since this area is not traveled as frequently as some of our other natural places around Las Vegas, it is advisable to notify someone of your travel plans in case of vehicle complications or trouble on the trail. A cell phone is not dependable in this area due to intermittent areas of coverage.

Although this area is a wildlife refuge, it is open for vehicular travel on approved and designated roads. Only street-legal vehicles are permitted on the refuge. Hiking, camping, backpacking, horseback riding, and some limited hunting activities are also allowed.

The western portion of the wildlife refuge is restricted from public access. The Nellis Air Force Base uses this section for training exercises. Obtain a map of the area at the field station for clarification of public access areas before journeying out onto the Desert National Wildlife Range.

1. Gass Peak

Round trip: 7 miles

Elevation range: 4900–6943 feet

Difficulty: Difficult

Hiking time: 4–6 hours

Best canine hiking seasons: Fall through spring

Under foot and paw: Loose shale rock (sometimes sharp), limestone outcrops, and dirt roads

Regulations: Dogs must be on a leash 6 feet long or less. Waste, including dog waste, must be removed and disposed of properly.

Map: USGS Gass Peak 7.5' quadrangle

Information: Desert National Wildlife Range, (702) 879-6110 (Note: If calling from Las Vegas, you must dial the area code), or *www.desertcomplex.fws.gov/desertrange/index.htm*

Water available: Seasonal spring

Getting there: This hike is located in the Desert National Wildlife Range. From Las Vegas, take US Highway 95 north. Approximately 15.3 miles past Ann Road, turn right onto the dirt road (unofficially known as Corn Creek Road) where signs direct you to the Desert National Wildlife Range. Follow the road for 4 miles to the Refuge office and self-serve information kiosk, which will be on the left side of the road. In front of the information kiosk, near the parking area, there is a "Sign In" booklet. Please sign in. This is a

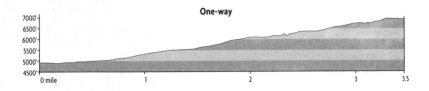

remote area and it is beneficial to have a record of your area of travel. Also, funding is based on visitor use, so it is helpful to the Range if you sign in. From the parking lot, proceed east a short distance to the T intersection. Turn right onto Mormon Well Road. Keep your eyes open because bighorn sheep are often spotted along Mormon Well Road. After 4 miles there is a dirt road to the right marked Gass Peak Road. Turn onto Gass Peak Road and proceed 8.1 miles to the trailhead. The trailhead is marked with a sign reading "Authorized Vehicles Only" and a small parking area. Park here.

Gass Peak offers solitude, a challenging trail, and excellent views of Las Vegas, the Sheep Mountains, the Las Vegas Range, and the Spring Mountains Range. This hike is an exciting change from populated, well-defined trails, but only experienced hikers with fit dogs should attempt it. Aside from the distance and elevation gain, the most challenging aspect of this trail is the lack of trail. For the majority of the hike, at best there is a user-created trail to follow. The hike is navigable, though, and if you pay attention to your surroundings, the route will guide you to incredible views on top of Gass Peak. It can be mentally challenging for your dog if you let it lead in front of you on the leash and find the best path around bushes, rocks, and other obstacles you may run across. Most of this adventure is on loose rocks, so dog booties may be appropriate if your dog has sensitive pads or nails that wear down easily.

Before you begin hiking, take a good look at the ridgelines between the trailhead and the summit. The route follows two ridgelines to the top of Gass Peak, where the large radio towers are located. The first ridgeline begins at the end of the dirt road and then connects with the main ridgeline that leads directly to Gass Peak. For a good portion of the way there is a faint user-created trail, and it is easy to lose it. Since following the ridgeline is fairly straightforward, once you understand the route you can let your dog lead the way. Most trails don't challenge a dog's mind, but this one will.

From the trailhead, begin hiking toward Gass Peak on the dirt road. Gass Peak is named after Octavius Decatur Gass, one of the founding fathers of Las Vegas. Octavius Gass is best known as the owner of the

Mormon Fort in downtown Las Vegas (after the Mormons left). While he is often remembered as a man with horrible luck—he failed at many endeavors throughout the course of his life—the mountain and the street in town are named after him, so his memory lives on!

After hiking a short distance, the dirt road forks to the left and right.

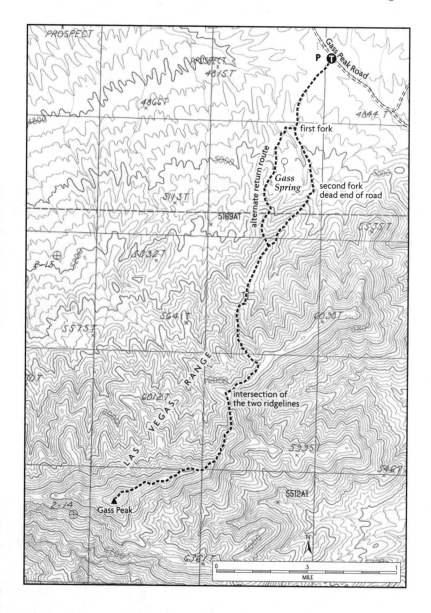

While both roads eventually take you to the same place, the road to the left will take you directly to the base of the first ridgeline. (The road to the right will take you past a seasonal spring, which can be visited on the return trip.) Not long after the fork, the dirt road abruptly comes to an end. There are two barely discernable trails, one straight ahead and one to the left. Take the trail to the left and begin the climb to the top of the ridgeline. At this point the trail will get rockier, so if your dog needs booties, now is a good time to put them on your dog's paws.

Follow the ridgeline up and down the saddles. After about 1.6 miles, the ridgeline meets a second ridgeline that leads directly to the top of Gass Peak. You will know when you get to this intersection because all of a sudden the ridgeline that obviously leads to the top of Gass Peak comes into view, just southeast of the ridgeline you have been following. Follow the saddle down to the left and climb up onto the second ridge. Note what the area looks like, so on your way back down you can follow the same ridgelines.

Once you are on the second ridge, follow it up to Gass Peak. Along the way are large limestone formations. Sometimes it is easier to walk on top of them, and sometimes at the base, so just use your judgment and do what is easiest on you and your doggie. Since there is more than one way to the top, just let your dog lead the way again and enjoy the

Camy and Mollie beg for goldfish crackers while Tracy eats her lunch near Gass Peak.

journey with incredible views. You four-legged friend should be having a blast by this time due to all the scrambling around rocks, sniffing for the trail, and weaving through bushes.

When you reach the top, which is 6943 feet above sea level, the view is one of the best in town. On a clear day the whole valley is laid out below, but best views are of the Spring Mountains Range and the Sheep Mountains. Since it is difficult to see these areas from any other point around town, Gass Peak offers a unique vantage point. Your dog may think it's a good idea to sniff around the solar panels and other equipment at the top of the peak, but try not to let it. You never know if any of the equipment may be loose or hazardous to your dog.

Once done at the top, return to your car (that little tiny speck down below) the way you came. Or, if you would like to take an alternate route past a seasonal spring, from the ridgeline closest to the trailhead, watch for a dirt road to the left. This is the road that you originally passed at the beginning of the hike. When you see the road, cut over to it. The road will pass a seasonal spring before meeting up with the main trail just before the parking lot.

2. Hidden Forest

Round trip: 10.2 miles
Elevation range: 5842–7855 feet
Difficulty: Moderate
Hiking time: 6 hours or overnight for a backpacking trip
Best canine hiking seasons: Spring through fall
Under foot and paw: Loose gravel and sand
Regulations: Dogs must be on a leash 6 feet long or less. Waste, including dog waste, must be removed and disposed of properly.
Map: USGS White Sage Flat, Black Hills, Sheep Peak, and Hayford Peak 7.5' quadrangles
Information: Desert National Wildlife Range, (702) 879-6110 (Note: If calling from Las Vegas, you must dial the area code), or *www.desertcomplex.fws.gov /desertrange/index.htm*
Water available: Spring

Getting there: This hike is located in the Desert National Wildlife Range. From Las Vegas take US Highway 95 north. Approximately 15.3 miles past Ann Road, turn right onto the dirt road (unofficially known as Corn Creek Road) where signs direct you to the Desert National Wildlife Range. Follow the road for 4 miles to the Refuge office and self-serve information kiosk, which will be on the left side of the road. In front of the information kiosk, near the parking area, there is a "Sign In" booklet. Please sign in. This is a remote area and it is beneficial to have a record of your area of travel. Also, funding is based on visitor use, so it is helpful to the Range if you sign in. From the parking lot, proceed east a short distance to the T intersection. Turn north (left) onto Alamo Road. After 16 miles turn east (right) onto Hidden Forest Road. A high-clearance vehicle is suggested for the Hidden Forest Road, but depending on recent weather conditions, a two-wheel drive vehicle should be sufficient. Contact a park ranger for current road conditions. Travel east for just under 4 miles to where the road is closed. The hike begins at this point, so park here. The trail leads up the canyon from the parking area on the closed road.

Do you and your dog love Mount Charleston but hate the crowds? If so, give Hidden Forest a try. This trail begins in open desert and climbs up into the pines, ending at an old log cabin and spring where the surroundings make you feel like you are in the Spring Mountains. Best of all, this area is not as commonly traveled, so solitude will be a welcome treat for you and your dog. If your pooch is a camping hound, this hike is suitable for a backpacking trip and an overnight adventure. This hike is only recommended for healthy, fit dogs. The loose gravel that makes up most of the hike can be more tiring than you might expect.

From the parking area, the Hidden Forest trail begins by heading up the canyon, past a gate and trailhead sign on the Hidden Forest road. (The distances given on the sign are inaccurate.) The trail is oriented generally west to east, with a steady incline. The first portion of the hike is through an upper desert plant community, primarily consisting of scrub bushes like creosote and white bursage. Keep in mind that this is the warmest portion of the hike, with little to no shade available. So if it's hot in Las Vegas, you and your dog will still be hot here. If the weather has been

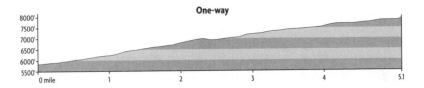

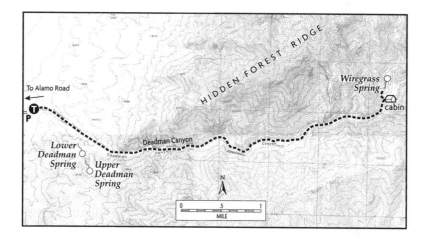

warm, wake your dog up early and set out on the hike before the sun is too high in the sky. If it has been cold out, your dog may need a doggie sweater to keep it warm. The elevation for this section of the trail is only in the 5000–6000 foot range.

After a short distance, the trail drops down into a wash that narrows and widens as you gain elevation at a gradual pace. After a little more than 1 mile, you and your dog will begin to move farther into the canyon, and the trail changes from an old roadbed to a pack trail. Under your feet and your dog's paws, the ground is primarily a soft gravel wash bottom with some remnants of the road visible from time to time. If your dog likes to be a sleuthhound, you can always try to solve the mystery of the canyon you are hiking into. The canyon is named Deadman Canyon. Unfortunately, the story of how the canyon got its name has long been lost, but it is reasonable to assume that a body was found in this canyon at some point in the past. So let your dog sniff the air. While sniffing for clues, your dog will also smell the change in vegetation. The plants growing in the canyon are a pinyon-juniper plant community, so there is a lot more shade here compared to the beginning of the hike.

As the trail continues, the canyon gradually narrows; the rocky walls twist and turn, keeping the trail interesting. Just over 3.3 miles into the hike, after a narrow section, the trail widens out and the first pine trees become visible. The canyon continues to widen and narrow, but the pine trees give shade, and the journey seems much more enjoyable. Continue hiking up through the mature ponderosa pines for about 2 more miles till you come to an old corral and log cabin.

Jasmine carries her own gear for this overnight trip.

The cabin is at the juncture of Deadman Canyon and an unnamed side canyon. This area is just shy of 8000 feet in elevation, so temperatures are cool and refreshing in the summertime. The cabin is unlocked and open for public use. There are limited supplies in the cabin—pots, pans, and sometimes canned food—and picnic tables outside. According to the U.S. Fish and Wildlife Service, the cabin was built in the 1910s or 1920s and used by bootleggers. From the cabin, follow a dirt trail to the north toward Wiregrass Spring for water. If you are standing at the door of the cabin looking out, the trail will be off to your right. The spring is approximately 0.13 mile from the cabin. Please remember that wildlife rely on this water source, so do not linger around the spring for too long and definitely do not camp right next to it. As always, it is advisable to filter the water.

If you and your dog are interested in an overnight backpacking experience, this is truly a great area to try. You can use the cabin, or pack in a tent if you prefer. Due to its infrequent use by humans, this cabin has been taken over by small mammals, so we do not recommend sleeping in it. The water available at the spring will need to be treated for human consumption, so bring along your water purifier or pack your own water. Do not camp near the water source; wildlife use this spring on a daily basis and need easy access to it. Also remember that at this elevation mountain storms are possible, so check weather reports and pack for colder temperatures if needed.

When it is time to go home, return the way you came. If your dog is carrying a backpack, pick up some litter from around the cabin that has appeared over the years and have your dog pack it out. It will be your pup's good deed for the day!

3. Joe May Canyon to Wildhorse Pass

Round trip: 8 miles
Elevation range: 4952–6878 feet
Difficulty: Moderate
Hiking time: 4 hours
Best canine hiking seasons: Spring and fall
Under foot and paw: Gravel wash
Regulations: Dogs must be on a leash 6 feet long or less. Waste, including dog waste, must be removed and disposed of properly.
Map: USGS Black Hills 7.5' quadrangle
Information: Desert National Wildlife Range, (702) 879-6110 (Note: If calling from Las Vegas, you must dial the area code), or *www.desertcomplex.fws.gov /desertrange/index.htm*
Water available: No

Getting there: This hike is located in the Desert National Wildlife Range. From Las Vegas, take US Highway 95 north. Approximately 15.3 miles past Ann Road, turn right onto the dirt road (unofficially known as Corn Creek Road) where signs direct you to the Desert National Wildlife Range. Follow the road for 4 miles to the Refuge office and self-serve information kiosk, which will be on the left side of the road. In front of the information kiosk, near the parking area, there is a "Sign In" booklet. Please sign in. This is a remote area and it is beneficial to have a record of your area of travel. Also, funding is based on visitor use, so it is helpful to the Range if you sign in. From the parking lot, proceed east a short distance to the T intersection. Turn left onto Alamo Road. After 3 miles turn east

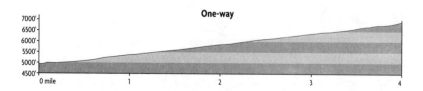

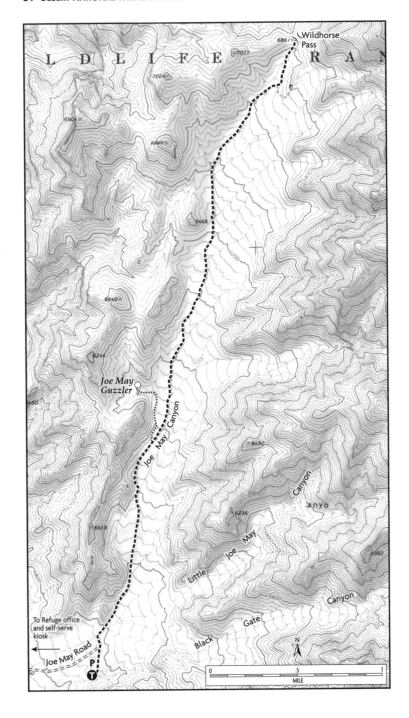

(right) onto Joe May Road (a high-clearance vehicle is suggested for this portion). After approximately 4 miles, there is a closed road to the north (left). Drive a short distance past the road and park near the corral. The trail begins on the closed road you passed with the "No vehicles" sign.

This hike will take you and your dog up a wide desert canyon, past a man-made guzzler, and to Wildhorse Pass. From the pass, you can see north into beautiful Picture Canyon. Without question, you will understand how this canyon got its name. Your dog will enjoy this trail because there

Rocket, always styling, wears a lei while hiking Joe May Canyon.

is a good chance of spotting wildlife here; animals are attracted to the man-made guzzler. If you do see wildlife, bighorn sheep in particular, remember to keep your distance. They are scared of you and your dog. The terrain throughout this hike is a typical gravel wash bottom and the elevation change is generally consistent throughout the hike. Washes are a bit more tiresome to walk through then harder surfaces, so make sure your dog is in good shape before setting off on this hike.

From the "No Vehicles" sign, begin by leading your dog up the old closed road in a very large wash running north and south. You will be hiking up the west side of Joe May Canyon at the base of tall limestone cliffs. To the east and northeast are several smaller canyons, including the Little Joe May and Black Gate Canyon. These canyons require some tough scrambling, and are not suitable for most dogs. The hike described here continues up Joe May Canyon, ending at a mountain pass. This hike is exposed with no real shade available, so save it for cooler days when shade is not necessary. Your dog will enjoy looking for lizards and birds as you walk along the wash.

This canyon was at one time accessible by road, but the road has been closed for decades. By following the wash and remnants of the old road up the canyon, you will easily reach the pass. After 1.5 miles, a small side canyon comes into view on the left. This canyon has a man-made water collection structure called a guzzler to maintain water for the local wildlife. To respect the wildlife in this area, do not venture up this canyon to the guzzler with your dog, but do take a minute to look around for bighorn sheep. If you are hiking with multiple people, have one or two people stay with the dogs while the others go look at the guzzler. From the intersection with the canyon that leads to the guzzler, continue straight ahead to the pass and the incredible views.

It is quite possible for you and your dog to see desert bighorn sheep in this area. The sheep are the size of small deer and blend in incredibly well to the desert landscape. The bighorn prefer to roam in small groups, primarily in rugged terrain.

By the time the soft gravel wash bottom starts to take its toll on you, and your dog no longer feels the need to roll around in it, you will be approaching Wildhorse Pass. As the trail gains elevation, the canyon beyond the pass stays just out of sight until you reach the top. The views beyond Wildhorse Pass and into the next canyon, Picture Canyon, are truly incredible. As you enjoy the beautiful, almost bowl-shaped terrain with its varied vegetation and rock formations, let your dog relax in some shade and build up energy for the return hike. This is an excellent spot to eat your lunch and let your dog devour a few doggie biscuits. After taking in the views, return to your vehicle via the route you came.

4. Long Valley

Round trip: 10 miles
Elevation range: 4989–7223 feet
Difficulty: Moderate
Hiking time: 5 hours
Best canine hiking seasons: Fall and spring
Under foot and paw: Gravel and some sharp rocks
Regulations: Dogs must be on a leash 6 feet long or less. Waste, including dog waste, must be removed and disposed of properly.
Map: USGS Gass Peak, Corn Creek Springs, Black Hills, and Sheep Peak 7.5' quadrangles
Information: Desert National Wildlife Range, (702) 879-6110 (Note: If calling from Las Vegas, you must dial the area code), or *www.desertcomplex.fws.gov/desertrange/index.htm*
Water available: No

Getting there: This hike is located in the Desert National Wildlife Range. From Las Vegas, take US Highway 95 north. Approximately 15.3 miles past Ann Road, turn right onto the dirt road (unofficially known as Corn Creek Road) where signs direct you to the Desert National Wildlife Range. Follow the road for 4 miles to the Refuge office and self-serve information kiosk, which will be on the left side of the road. In front of the information kiosk, near the parking area, there is a "Sign In" booklet. Please sign in. This is a remote area and it is beneficial to have a record of your area of travel. Also, funding is based on visitor use, so it is helpful

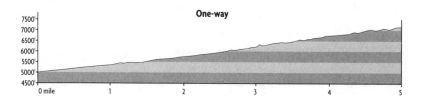

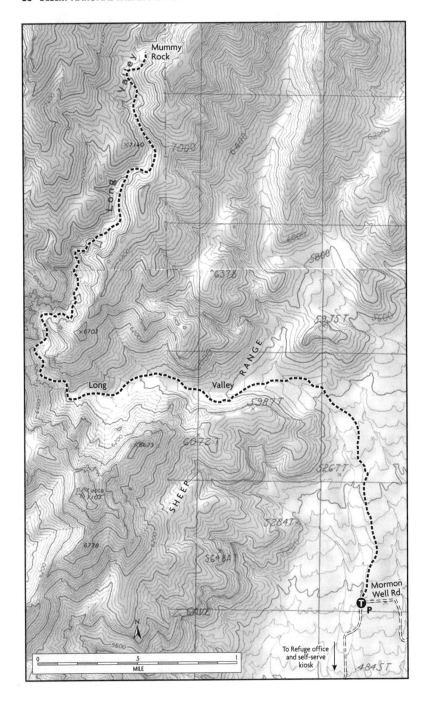

to the Range if you sign in. From the parking lot, proceed east a short distance to the T intersection. Turn right onto Mormon Well Road. Keep your eyes open because bighorn sheep are often spotted along Mormon Well Road. After about 9 miles there is a dirt turnaround and parking area on the left and the main road makes a sharp right turn. Park your car in the parking area. This is the trailhead.

This trail provides a hidden treat for any hiker and dog. From the parking area, the hike looks like it may be desolate and dry, but turn a corner farther up the canyon and there are junipers and pines along narrow canyon walls. The seclusion alone is worth the trip, but the added treat of a varied landscape and a lot of shade makes this a rewarding trip for you and your dog.

For dogs with sensitive paws, definitely pack the dog booties. The rock that makes up much of the terrain can be hard on the paws. This trail can be lengthened or shortened as desired. Although the trail described here is a 10-mile round-trip ramble, the narrow portion of the Long Valley Canyon begins after 2.6 miles. So if a little shade and a quick walk in a fun new area is all you need, you can quit here and complete the hike in just over 5 miles. Conversely, the canyon continues past the area described as the end of the hike; so for the more athletic pooches and their owners, it is possible to continue farther up the canyon. This area isn't called Long Valley for nothing! Make sure you and your dog have the water and energy to make the return trip. Carrying a dog out of a canyon is no fun! Since this hike takes you and your dog deep into a canyon, check the weather forecast before you begin hiking to make sure rains and flash floods are not predicted.

The trail begins at the parking area along the closed road overlooking the wash. As you hike up the road toward Long Valley, take note of the vegetation that surrounds you and your dog. The trail leads through a large Joshua tree forest. This is not what we may think of as a traditional forest, but it is full of character nonetheless. Joshua trees thrive only at certain elevations with specific amounts of annual rainfall, so for this forest to be thriving as it is, all conditions must be right. The smaller plants mixed in among the Joshua trees with sharp, green swordlike leaves are the yuccas. Native Americans have used the fibers for these leaves to make sandals and baskets. Do not let your dog get too close to a yucca, or it might get a prick in the nose!

Follow the dirt road for approximately 2 miles until the road begins

Mummy man rock in Long Valley canyon

to move away to the right from the wash. At this point drop down into the wash. The rest of the hike is up the canyon wash, without an evident trail. Under feet and paws, the ground is a typical wash bottom with soft gravel that gives your legs a good workout.

One of the great treats for you and your dog on this hike is the sudden change from the ordinary to the extraordinary. As you hike farther into Long Valley and look uphill, the terrain appears to be more of the same. As you near what appears to be the back of the canyon, the landscape changes dramatically with the introduction of juniper and pine trees. After 2.6 miles the canyon turns sharply to the north (right) and immediately narrows. The canyon walls become intermittently steep with completely vertical formations and interspersed trees along the canyon bottom and up the slopes. There is abundant shade available for a rest stop or lunch. Your dog will enjoy a nice pause here.

As you continue up the canyon, the canyon narrows, then widens, then narrows again. There is shade available throughout the remainder of the hike. In several areas you and your dog will see large boulders in the middle of the wash that found their home here when flood waters carried them down the canyon.

When you have fulfilled your hiking experience you may return at any time. For those who wish to continue, follow the canyon as it winds around back and forth. Approximately 5 miles into the hike, look for a rock formation in the middle of the canyon loosely resembling a mummy (see photo). This is the end of this hike as described here. Return the way you came or, if you would like to continue up the canyon, feel free.

5. Mormon Well

Round trip: 0.7 mile
Elevation range: 6327–6520 feet
Difficulty: Easy
Hiking time: 0.5 hour
Best canine hiking seasons: Year-round
Under foot and paw: Dirt, gravel, flattened bushes
Regulations: Dogs must be on a leash 6 feet long or less. Waste, including dog waste, must be removed and disposed of properly. This area is listed on the National Register of Historical Places; do not alter or remove any artifacts or structure material.
Map: USGS Mormon Well 7.5' quadrangle
Information: Desert National Wildlife Range, (702) 879-6110 (Note: If calling from Las Vegas, you must dial the area code), or *www.desertcomplex.fws.gov/desertrange/index.htm*
Water available: Spring flowing into containment area

Getting there: This hike is located in the Desert National Wildlife Range. From Las Vegas, take US Highway 95 north. Approximately 15.3 miles past Ann Road, turn right onto the dirt road (unofficially known as Corn Creek Road) where signs direct you to the Desert National Wildlife Range. Follow the road for 4 miles to the Refuge office and self-serve information kiosk, which will be on the left side of the road. In front of the infor-

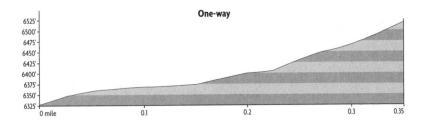

mation kiosk, near the parking area, there is a "Sign In" booklet. Please sign in. This is a remote area and it is beneficial to have a record of your area of travel. Also, funding is based on visitor use, so it is helpful to the Range if you sign in. From the parking lot, proceed east a short distance to the T intersection. Turn right onto Mormon Well Road. Keep your eyes open because bighorn sheep are often spotted along Mormon Well Road. After 25.2 miles, turn into and park in the cleared dirt area on the right side of the road. There is a dry, concrete water trough in this area. The trailhead is on the east side of the parking area.

This hike requires a lot of scenic driving for a relatively short hike, but sometimes that is just what we're in the mood for, and just what our couch-potato dogs can handle. However, the trail is close to two other hikes, Long Valley and Sawmill Canyon, making it possible to hike multiple trails in one day. Regardless of how many miles you intend to hike, you and your dog will enjoy this trail. For the people in the group there is an interesting historical aspect of the hike, and for the dogs there are a lot of bushes to weave through and around on the way to a spring. Listed on the National Register of Historical Places, the Mormon Well area was used during the 1700s by Paiute Indians. Later, it served as a stopping-place for pioneers passing through in the late 1800s to early 1900s, and as a holding spot for livestock. Remnants of structures used for ranching can still be seen. Due to the place's historical significance, removal of artifacts or disturbance to any structures is strictly prohibited. If a day of driving with a short hike is in your cards, definitely pack a picnic because this is a great area for relaxing.

From the parking area, guide your dog southeast up an old road. After 0.09 mile the road will intersect another dirt road. At the intersection, turn left and follow the road up the hillside. After a short distance, a corral will be visible on the right side of the road. There is a gate on the side of the corral facing the road. Walk through the gate and continue across the corral and out the other side through another gate. Desert shrubs have grown inside the corral since it has not been in use for a long time. Your dog will have fun weaving through the maze-like vegetation to the other side of the corral. If your dog has a long coat, you may want to give it a once-over after you have passed through the bushes to make sure no burrs or prickers are stuck to the fur. Another pointer: if you have a dog with short legs, it may be best to carry it through the corral. If you have an adventurous dog that needs to be challenged mentally, have one person hold the dog at the first entrance while a second person walks around the outside of the corral toward the second entrance. Set the dog free inside the corral and see if your dog can find its way out the second entrance to reach you.

The spring is located just beyond the southern gate of the corral. From the gate walk straight and follow one of the several side trails leading through the brush to the hillside on the left. The water from the

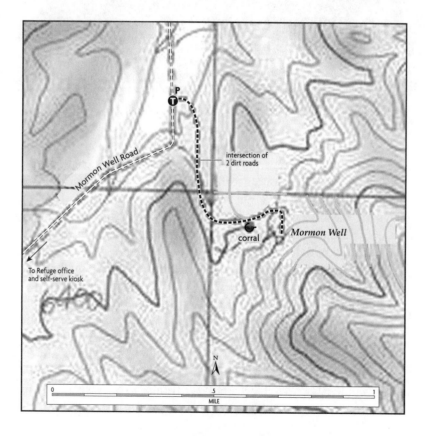

The spring at Mormon Well flows into this water catchment.

spring is stored in a water enclosure at ground level, just at the base of
the hillside. It is advisable that you check the water before letting your
dog get a drink or jump in. Since the water is collected in an enclosure, it
can be stagnant if there has not been much water flowing into it. When
stagnant, the water becomes black and less than desirable, and your dog
shouldn't drink it or play in it. Regardless of the water quality, you and
your dog will find that it still is a fun place to explore.

When you are finished checking out the spring and the corral, return
to your car, play fetch a few times, and exit the parking area to the left
to return along the road the way you came in. For more of an adventure,
you can continue driving north on Mormon Well Road. Eventually the
road exits the Desert National Wildlife Range and intersects US Highway
93 north of Apex. To return to Las Vegas, turn south (right) onto US
Highway 93 and proceed to the intersection with Interstate 15. Drive
south on Interstate 15 to Las Vegas. It is advisable to carry a map of your
entire trip if you choose this option.

6. Sawmill Canyon

Round trip: 10.8 miles*
Elevation range: 5496–8184 feet
Difficulty: Difficult
Hiking time: 6 hours or overnight for a backpacking trip
Best canine hiking seasons: Spring through fall
Under foot and paw: Dirt road and gravel washes
Regulations: Dogs must be on a leash 6 feet long or less. Waste, including dog waste, must be removed and disposed of properly.
Map: USGS Mormon Well and Hayford Peak 7.5' quadrangles
Information: Desert National Wildlife Range, (702) 879-6110 (Note: If calling from Las Vegas, you must dial the area code), or *www.desertcomplex.fws.gov /desertrange/index.htm*
Water available: Spring flowing into containment area

*10 with four-wheel-drive vehicle

Getting there: This hike is located in the Desert National Wildlife Range. From Las Vegas, take US Highway 95 north. Approximately 15.3 miles past Ann Road, turn right onto the dirt road (unofficially known as Corn Creek Road) where signs direct you to the Desert National Wildlife Range. Follow the road for 4 miles to the Refuge office and self-serve information kiosk, which will be on the left side of the road. In front of the information kiosk, near the parking area, there is a "Sign In" booklet. Please sign in. This is a remote area and it is beneficial to have a record of your area of travel. Also, funding is based on visitor use, so it is helpful to the Range if you sign in. From the parking lot, proceed east a short distance to the T intersection. Turn right onto Mormon Well Road. Keep your eyes open because bighorn sheep are often spotted along Mormon Well Road. After 30.5 miles, a dirt road intersects the main road from the left. This is the road to turn left on, but please note that there is an immediate steep hill

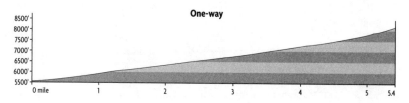

to ascend in your vehicle. Before you reach the trailhead there is a steep, rocky descent as well. If you are without a four-wheel-drive vehicle or you don't feel comfortable navigating through difficult sections of road, park off to the side of the road and begin your hike here. If you continue, drive up the hill and follow the dirt road until you reach large boulders and a gate that blocks the road beyond it. Park your vehicle here. From the main road it is about 0.4 mile to the gate.

Do you have a mutt that loves sleeping in a tent? Sawmill Canyon is a remote hike with a great camping area that includes a water source. Regardless of whether you do this trail as a day hike or an overnight trip, you and your dog will find it to be an instant favorite! The trail follows an old roadbed which has been blocked for decades, so almost any dog that can handle the distance would make a great companion on this adventure. The canyon boasts all the elements of a rewarding trip: diverse vegetation so the sniffer never gets bored, shade for resting, a water source for drinking, and a place to put up a tent and absorb the solitude. Please note that the trail itself is not particularly challenging, but its length and a steady grade make it a moderately difficult hike, especially if you are carrying a pack.

From the gate, begin the hike by leading your dog up the old dirt road. The road moves in and out of washes and small drainages but overall is

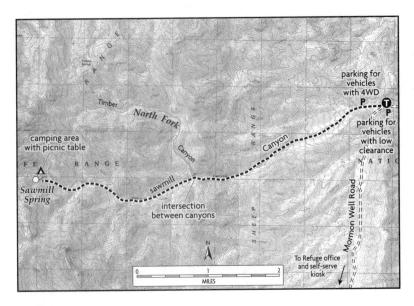

Where's lunch? Are the hot dogs ready yet?

quite intact, with easy footing for you and your dog. At the beginning of the hike, the elevation is at approximately 5500 feet. The vegetation is upland desert, with the beautiful Joshua tree as a resident. In the spring, flowers are abundant on the bushes and small plants in the area, so let your dog sniff the air. Many of the bushes turn to a golden brown in the fall months, particularly the rabbitbrush, which is plentiful on both sides of the trail. As the elevation increases, the Joshua trees disappear and the junipers come into view. In the fall, these junipers will be chock-full of small blue-grey berries. The trail steadily moves uphill in a slow rolling manner. Over the duration of the hike, the trail gains just over 2600 feet in elevation.

After hiking for about 3 miles, you and your dog will get to a fork in the road. The left fork leads to Sawmill Canyon and is marked with a small sign that says "25." The right fork leads to the North Fork and Timber Canyon. Take the path to the left, continuing up Sawmill Canyon. As the name of the canyon indicates, this area was once the home of a working sawmill. Removal of any artifacts is strictly prohibited. Ponderosa pines from the canyon were logged and transported to local settlements for development. Along the trail, remnants of previous human occupation are common, such as water piping and lumber. Just past the fork in the trail, you and your dog will encounter a large pile of lumber. Since there may be nails in the boards, it is best to keep your dog from climbing on the pile.

For the next 2 miles the trail leads through a beautiful canyon with rolling, tall hillsides visible just beyond either side of the canyon. Since this portion of the trail is substantially higher in elevation than the start of the hike, the vegetation is quite different. Let your dog climb up and walk on some of the downed trees in the white fir and pine tree community.

About 5.4 miles into the hike, the trail ends in a small bowl-shaped area at the end of the canyon. The road slowly disappears from view while hugging the south (left) side of the canyon. At the end of the trail is a picnic table and fire circle, which makes for an excellent camping spot large enough for ten or more tents. To the left there is a more established fire structure that would be suitable for cooking for large groups. If you have a group of hiking friends that like to take their dogs, definitely consider camping here. It is a perfect area for playing fetch with your dog as well. The ground is soft dirt, so your dog will be comfortable running around and rolling in the dirt.

Just beyond the campsite is a water source. The water is piped down from the hillside to a small water-holding container. The water is not suitable for drinking directly and should be purified before use. Many wild creatures use this water source as well, so do not camp close to it. Instead, camp back in the main area by the picnic table. This allows wild animals to approach and drink the water without being frightened away. This camping area is at an elevation of approximately 8100 feet, so dress and pack for cooler weather and for sudden weather changes.

Once you are done enjoying this area and your dog has rested up for the return hike, return to your car by retracing your footsteps.

LAKE MEAD NATIONAL RECREATION AREA

The Lake Mead National Recreation Area (NRA) was the first national recreation area ever to be established. Its creation in 1964 set aside 1.5 million acres along the Colorado River for recreation as well as for preservation of these lands. There are over 550 miles of shoreline in the Lake Mead NRA. Although generally thought of for its water resources and recreation, only 13 percent of the park is water; the remaining acreage is land. And with over a million acres of land, there are plenty of hiking opportunities available.

The terrain in the park varies greatly, from flat desert to rocky mountains, with elevations ranging from 517 to over 7000 feet. The park belongs to a unique area where three different desert types converge: the Sonoran, the Mojave, and the Great Basin.

The incredible geologic, biologic, and environmental diversity here ensures an assortment of hiking experiences. Different trails here lead to mountain tops, beautiful desert flats, and down canyons to the Colorado River, just to name a few.

The Lake Mead NRA serves as a safe haven for a number of plant and animal species. These species have suffered loss of habitat outside of the recreation area due to human development. Examples include the desert bighorn sheep, the Yuma clapper rail, the banded Gila monster, the desert tortoise, and the California bear paw poppy. To make sure your visit does not harm these species, several steps must be taken. First, stay on approved roads and trails. Many previously open areas have been closed to travel due to the presence of sensitive species. By adhering to the land-use restrictions in place, you can give these species the best possible chance to survive and thrive. Secondly, as required by the Lake Mead NRA, dogs must be kept on leash at all times. Many species, such as the desert bighorn, view dogs as predators. Having dogs off leash can affect the bighorn by putting undue stress on the herd. Added stress can lead to increased disease, injury, and in some cases death.

Temperatures at Lake Mead can commonly be 5–10°F hotter than in the Las Vegas Valley. Keep this in mind when planning a trip to this area. These warmer temperatures make the Lake Mead area a prime location for winter hikes.

Please note: The Lake Mead NRA requires a fee for entrance. The entrance fee for a car is $5.00; an annual pass can be purchased for $20.00.

7. Bluffs Trail

Round trip: 1.8 miles
Elevation range: 1273–1363 feet
Difficulty: Easy
Hiking time: 1.5 hours
Best canine hiking seasons: Fall through spring
Under foot and paw: Dirt
Regulations: Fee area. Dogs must be on a leash 6 feet long or less at all times. Waste must be removed and disposed of properly.
Map: USGS Henderson 7.5' quadrangle
Information: National Park Service, Alan Bible Visitor Center, (702) 293-8990 and (702) 293-8997, or *www.nps.gov/lame*
Water available: No

Getting there: This hike is located by Las Vegas Bay, within the Lake Mead National Recreation Area. From Henderson, take Lake Mead Drive east to

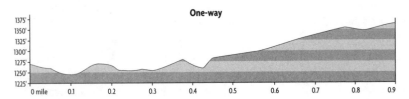

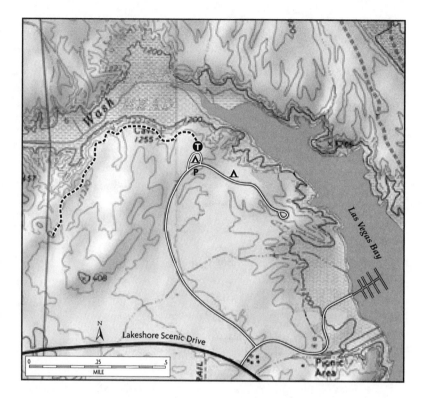

the lake. From the intersection with Boulder Highway, the fee station is
6.8 miles east. From the fee station, drive approximately 2 miles and turn
left into the Las Vegas Bay area. Lake Mead Drive turns into Lakeshore
Scenic Drive as you enter the recreation area. Make another left, following the signs for the campground. Park at the campground kiosk on the
right side of the road. The trailhead is located along the outer perimeter
of the campground, to the north (left), between campground spaces 72
and 74. Follow the sign for the campground trail and amphitheater.

Traveling along the bluffs above Las Vegas Wash, this hike is all about the
scenery. The well-defined trail takes the hiker from the mouth of Las Vegas
Bay up the Las Vegas Wash, ending at the top of a moderate knoll with 360-
degree views. Your dog will enjoy the view below and the well-maintained
trail. This is an exposed hike without any access to the water below, so
make sure water bottles are full and the temperature is mild. If you set out
to hike this trail in the morning, be advised that park rangers lead groups
of schoolchildren on field trips here. If your doggie does not do well with

Mimi has little legs, a big attitude, and a love for the trail.

children, you may want to have an alternate route selected in advance.

The Bluffs trail is well-maintained with a rock border along both sides. It passes a small outdoor amphitheater on its way due north toward the Las Vegas Wash. When nearing the wash, the trail turns west (left) and follows the top of the bluffs lining the wash below.

The flow of water in the Las Vegas Wash can vary greatly throughout the year. The wash carries urban runoff, treated sewage, and shallow groundwater from the city out to Lake Mead. (Less than 5 percent of the water in Lake Mead comes from the Las Vegas Wash; the Colorado River is the major source of water entering Lake Mead.) The wash offers much-needed habitat for wetland birds and other species. It also cleans the water, removing pollutants before it reaches Lake Mead.

Over the past decade, an enormous amount of work has been put into preserving and enhancing the Las Vegas Wash wetland habitat. What once was a dumping ground for trash has now been cleaned up with the public's help and brought back to a healthy natural state. Non-native invasive plant species have been removed, and native plants reintroduced. The stream flow was altered to enhance retention time and reduce soil erosion along the banks.

Your dog will enjoy the view below with birds wading in the shallow waters and the occasional fish jumping out of the water. The trail is very well-marked and -maintained, making it easy on the doggie paws. Although this trail is used for school groups, it is not otherwise well-publicized, so chances are you and your pooch may be alone on this hike, especially on the weekends or in the afternoon.

From the highest point of the bluff, there are fantastic views of the wash below. Keep on the lookout for the creatures that make this wash their home. There are many species of waterfowl and shorebirds and it is not uncommon to see waders such as great blue herons, green herons, great egrets, and snowy egrets fishing the waters below. Over 125 different bird species have been sighted along the Las Vegas Wash. As the trail moves away from the wash, it turns to the southwest and ascends a hill. The trail continues up to the top of the hill for fantastic views of the area in all directions. Retrace your steps back to the campground and your vehicle.

8. Bowl of Fire

Round trip: 9.8 miles*
Elevation range: 1696–2261 feet
Difficulty: Moderate
Hiking time: 5 hours
Best canine hiking seasons: Fall through spring
Under foot and paw: Gravel, dirt, and rocks
Regulations: Fee area. Dogs must be on a leash 6 feet long or less at all times. Waste must be removed and disposed of properly.
Map: USGS Callville Bay 7.5' quadrangle
Information: National Park Service, Alan Bible Visitor Center, (702) 293-8990 and (702) 293-8997, or *www.nps.gov/lame*
Water available: No

*The first portion of the hike (approximately 3 miles) can be driven with a four-wheel-drive vehicle (the gravel can get soft). The hike is then 4 miles round trip, with a hiking time of 2 hours.

Getting there: This hike is located near Callville Bay, within Lake Mead National Recreation Area. From Henderson, take Lake Mead Drive east. From the intersection with Boulder Highway, the fee station is 6.8 miles

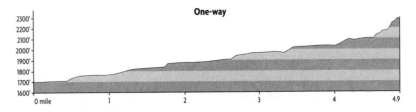

to the east. Just past the fee station, take a left onto Northshore Road. (Alternate directions: From the north side of the valley, take Lake Mead Boulevard east over Sunrise Mountain, past the fee station, to the intersection with Northshore Road.) Turn north (left) onto Northshore Road and then make a left at mile marker 16. If you have a low-clearance vehicle, or if you choose to hike the entire 9.8 miles, park on the left in the open unpaved area. If you have a vehicle with four-wheel drive you can continue almost 3 miles, parking farther up Callville Wash off the side of the road.

Who says all the beautiful red sandstone is at Red Rock Canyon? The Bowl of Fire trail takes you from a seemingly ordinary wash to unusual red Aztec sandstone formations. The area didn't get its name by being mundane; this area is truly one of the most gorgeous spots in the Lake Mead region. Lake Mead can get quite warm, so venture out only when the temperatures are practical for hiking. On a rare occasion you may find water in sandstone depressions called *tinajas*, but do not count on it for your drinking water. Dogs will enjoy the change from sauntering up a wash to the treat of a little scramble at the end of the hike. If your dog has sensitive paws, you may want to take a pair of dog booties with you on this hike. The sandstone formations have a texture similar to sandpaper, and may wear down the nails and pads of your dog—more so than other hikes described in this book.

From the parking area just off the Northshore Road, walk on the dirt road up Callville Wash. After 0.3 mile, a side road to the left will appear. This road leads to Lovell Canyon (Hike 15). Continue on the main road up Callville Wash. The Bowl of Fire Wash is 2.8 miles up the canyon from the parking area, on the north (left) side of the wash. If you have driven to this point, park at the entrance of the wash.

The hike follows the wash bottom as it curves back and forth, generally heading north. The wash substrate is gravel and sand. After 0.8 mile, the wash splits. Lead your dog to the left. As you hike, the beautiful Bowl of

Fire formation will come into view. In general, the trail begins to the west (left), circles the formation around the back side, ascends to an excellent vantage point that looks back down at the wash, then returns along the same path back to the car.

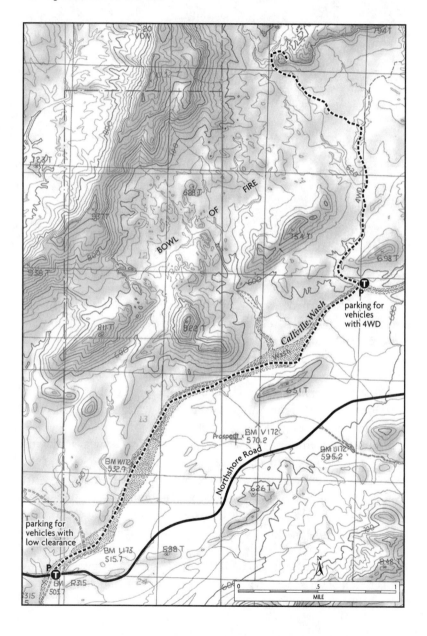

Striking views and red sandstone formations of the Bowl of Fire

As you near the red rock, continue around the base of the formation to the left side. This is where the fun begins. The trail continues up the first accessible side canyon on the right side. This portion of the trail requires a bit of rock scrambling in places, so let your dog have fun finding the way. In rainy seasons, there is water in the *tinajas* (natural depressions in the sandstone) in this area. Depending on how recently it has rained, and how much, there might even be enough water for dogs to splash around in, or at least get their feet wet.

As the trail continues, it takes another right turn up a hill to the top of the ridge. From the top, you are treated with incredible views of the whole area. Watch your dog in this area; there are steep drop-offs to the south. The Aztec sandstone that you see all around you is about 180 million years old. The sandstone outcrop was formed when rocks below the surface folded up and the Aztec sandstone—ancient petrified sand dunes—was pushed to the surface. The formations, canyons, and washes that you and your dog explore on this hike were created by weathering and erosion of the sandstone. When you are finished enjoying the views, return the way you came.

9. Boy Scout Canyon

Round trip: 7.4 miles*
Elevation range: 1400–2200 feet
Difficulty: Difficult
Hiking time: 5–6 hours
Best canine hiking seasons: Fall through spring
Under foot and paw: Sand, gravel, large boulders
Regulations: Fee area. Dogs must be on a leash 6 feet long or less at
  all times. Waste must be removed and disposed of properly.
Map: USGS Boulder City 7.5' quadrangle
Information: National Park Service, Alan Bible Visitor Center,
  (702) 293-8990 and (702) 293-8997, or *www.nps.gov/lame*
Water available: No

*6.2 miles with a vehicle with high clearance

Getting there: This hike is located just outside Boulder City, within Lake
Mead National Recreation Area. To get there, take US Highway 95/93
south from Las Vegas. After passing through Henderson, US Highway
95 will split away from US Highway 93, 1 mile past the Railroad Pass
Casino. Continue on US Highway 93 toward Boulder City. As you enter
Boulder City, turn right at Buchanan, which is the second stoplight. Drive
0.4 mile to Adams and turn left. Then drive 1.4 miles to Utah Street and
turn right. Continue 0.6 mile and turn left on the dirt road between the
powerline poles. The dirt road is wide and well-graded. It is suitable for
low-clearance cars. This road passes a power substation after about 1.5
miles. After approximately 2.7 miles there will be a faint dirt road on
the right. Roughly 200 feet past the faint dirt road is a second dirt road,
which is Approved Road 75D (AR 75D). If you are in a low-clearance vehicle, park off the main dirt road near the large power pole across from
the turnoff for AR 75D. This will be your trailhead, and where the hike

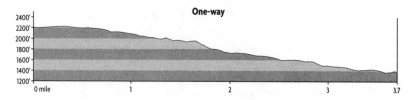

description starts. If you are in a vehicle with high clearance, turn onto AR 75D and continue down AR 75D for about 0.6 mile to the entrance of the canyon. Parking is available to the left. This will reduce your hiking distance by about 1.2 miles round trip.

Boy Scout Canyon is one of the reasons why hiking in Lake Mead National Recreation Area can be so wonderful. Few people know about this trail, so it is just the place to get away from it all. It offers beautiful wildflowers in the springtime, pictographs, challenging climbing areas for both you and your dog, and a variety of surroundings. Please note that this hike should only be attempted if your dog is in good physical condition and has tough paw pads. Doggie booties are highly recommended.

The trail begins at the intersection of the main dirt road and AR 75D. Hike approximately 0.6 miles in on AR 75D to the mouth of the canyon. Pass the cleared parking area to the left side of the canyon mouth and continue hiking into the canyon. Once in the canyon, follow the wash downhill. The canyon widens and narrows and there are many dry waterfalls along the way. At the first significant dry waterfall, look around on the rocks above you. There are numerous pictographs in the area. (Don't fret if you miss them, as it is often easier to see them on the return trip.) If you hike the trail in early spring, you will have the pleasure of being surrounded by desert marigolds, which are prolific throughout

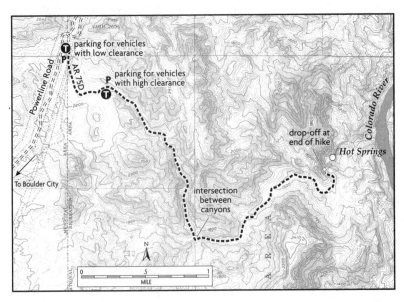

Mollie looks out over the drop-off at the end of the trail.

the wash. Globe mallow, California buckwheat, and brittlebush are also found along the way.

The first 2 miles of the trail can be very challenging for a dog or a novice hiker. There are plenty of large boulders and cliffs to climb up or around. While they are fun physical and mental challenges for a well-trained dog, they can create problems for dogs that have short legs, are out of shape, or have soft pads. Doggie booties are a definite plus on this hike. With that said, climbing up and around the rocks within the wash is a lot of fun. If your dog acts like it is part billy goat, this is definitely the hike for you. There are several smaller side canyons that join the main canyon; make sure to stay in the main wash as you work your way downhill.

After approximately 2 miles the canyon ends and the trail reaches a junction with three other canyons. There are several sets of tire tracks heading south from here, made by vehicles going off-road driving from a rifle range that is located down the canyon. Proceed by hiking down the far left canyon, which leads in the direction of the Colorado River. For the rest of the hike, the trail is a large wide wash. The gravel is small and loose. This area is a good place to watch for wildlife, including bighorn sheep. Approximately 3.5 miles into the hike, the trail will end abruptly at a dry waterfall that drops several hundred feet. Expect the drop-off when the walls of the canyon get extremely narrow. There is usually an enjoyable breeze at this spot on the trail, so if you have good control of your dog, let it stand at the top of the dry waterfall with its ears flapping in the breeze. While there is a route around the drop-off point (accessed by a small trail that leads north off the main one before you reach the dry waterfall), it is not recommended when you are hiking with your dog because there are steep drop-offs and it is all too easy for you to lose your stance and fall when helping your dog scramble. Return back up the wash the way you came.

10. Callville

Round trip: 2 miles
Elevation range: 1244–1382 feet
Difficulty: Easy
Hiking time: 1 hour
Best canine hiking seasons: Fall through spring
Under foot and paw: Dirt and sand
Regulations: Fee area. Dogs must be on a leash 6 feet long or less at all times. Waste must be removed and disposed of properly.
Map: USGS Callville Bay 7.5' quadrangle
Information: National Park Service, Alan Bible Visitor Center, (702) 293-8990 and (702) 293-8997, or *www.nps.gov/lame*
Water available: Access to Lake Mead

Getting there: This hike is located near Callville Bay, within Lake Mead National Recreation Area. From Henderson, take Lake Mead

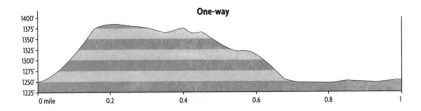

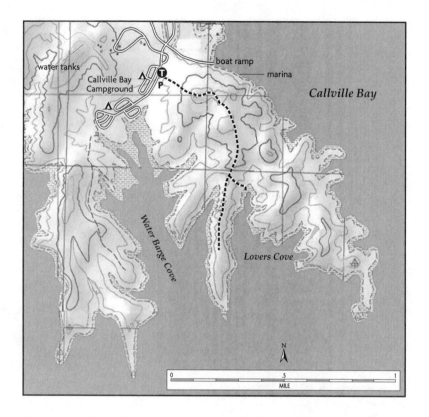

Drive east. From the intersection with Boulder Highway, the fee station is 6.8 miles to the east. Just past the fee station, take a left onto Northshore Road. (Alternate directions: From the north side of the valley, take Lake Mead Boulevard east over Sunrise Mountain, past the fee station, to the intersection with Northshore Road.) Go north on Northshore Road 8 miles, and then turn right toward Callville Bay. After 3.5 miles turn right, following the signs for the RV sewage dump area near the Callville Bay Campground. After 0.1 mile, just past the RV sewage dump, park on the left in an unpaved parking area next to the road.

If your dog likes the water, this is a quick trail with easy access to the lake. The hike is a short jaunt down to Lake Mead for some dog paddling, with the added bonus of great views. Just west of the marina, the trail travels from a small peak across a high section of desert and down to two protected coves to the south and southwest. The northeast side

According to Mia, frequent rests and water breaks are necessary.

of the point, near the marina, has more boat traffic and is not recommended for doggie swimming. The trail begins at the unpaved parking area and heads straight up the hillside to the east. The first portion of the hike is the steepest, going up 130 feet in 0.2 mile. There are some areas of loose rock, so tread carefully. At the top of this little peak (1382 feet in elevation), views are a full 360 degrees for miles in all directions. From the peak, follow the trail down the back side, heading south. The trail is met by several small side trails along the way, leading to higher vantage points or out to the water to the north. Continue on the main trail as it meanders over hills, down into little washes, and across the desert toward the south.

As you look over this vast landscape, try to picture steamboats moving across the water with the desert as their backdrop. Does the image seem out of place? In the late 1800s there was a big push to use the Colorado River for moving freight from the Gulf of California up into the interior of the Southwest. The idea never got fully off the ground; there were several tricky sections of the Colorado River that made steamboat travel challenging if not impossible. In fact, bolts were drilled into the canyon walls and cables were used to literally pull the steamships up difficult stretches of the Colorado River. (Today, dams restrict travel along the river.) The actual town of Callville was flooded when the Colorado River was dammed and Lake Mead was formed, but the marina and surrounding area still carry its name.

The trail continues up on a hill moving out to a point. Continue to the point for a spectacular view. If getting wet is your objective (or your dog's), there are side trails leading down to Lovers Cove on the east (left) side, or Water Barge Cove on the west (right) side of the point. Either cove provides great swimming; the water is typically warmer and calmer in the coves. Reserve some time for swimming, as your doggie may not want to leave this area. Return the way you came.

11. Cottonwood Spring

Round trip: 2.1 miles
Elevation range: 1937–2125 feet
Difficulty: Easy
Hiking time: 1 hour
Best canine hiking seasons: Fall through spring
Under foot and paw: Dirt and gravel
Regulations: Fee area. Dogs must be on a leash 6 feet long or less at all times. Waste must be removed and disposed of properly.
Map: USGS Callville Bay 7.5' quadrangle
Information: National Park Service, Alan Bible Visitor Center, (702) 293-8990 and (702) 293-8997, or *www.nps.gov/lame*
Water available: No

Getting there: This hike is located near Callville Bay, within Lake Mead National Recreation Area. From Henderson, take Lake Mead Drive east.

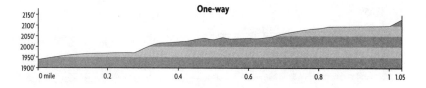

From the intersection with Boulder Highway, the fee station is 6.8 miles to the east. Just past the fee station, take a left onto Northshore Road. (Alternate directions: From the north side of the valley, take Lake Mead Boulevard east over Sunrise Mountain, past the fee station, and then turn left onto Northshore Road.) Go north on Northshore Road to mile marker 18, and then make a left and park at the pullout.

This peaceful hike follows a wash down to a couple of cottonwood trees, from which the spring got its name. Your four-legged friend will be sad to learn that the spring is usually dry. However, it is not uncommon to see the efforts of local animals digging down in the sand to reach water. Although there probably will not be any water at the spring, the cottonwood trees provide a wonderful respite for lunch with shade. If your dog feels the need to roll around in the gravel, this is a great spot for some serious rolling.

From the pullout where you parked, cross the Northshore Road to the obvious trailhead. Watch carefully for traffic; there is a turn in the road to the east that makes it difficult to see in that direction. The trail moves across the open desert to the south where it drops down into a wash. The first portion of this trail is clearly lined with rocks

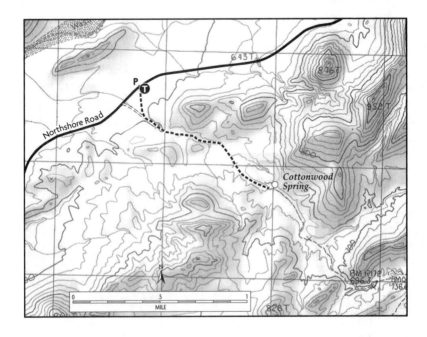

on either side. In the wash, the trail is not always evident, but by continuing down the wash to the southeast, you will get where you need to go.

Along the trail, the canyon wall formations and local plant life keep the hike interesting. Check out the barrel cactus on the north side of the wash. They are in such abundance and they seem to defy gravity as they grow out of small cracks and crevices in the canyon walls. This cactus was used by early Native Americans for a variety of purposes, including medicine (a pain reliever was made from it) as well as storage, using the hollowed-out "barrel." The seeds, flowers, fruit, and flesh were all eaten. Native Americans in the Southwest have used cottonwood trees as well. Carved kachina dolls are commonly made out of cottonwood trees, and the tree has medicinal uses.

There's no such thing as too small to hike.

Continuing down the wash, Cottonwood Spring is clearly evident. The two cottonwood trees that seem a bit out of place in this desert landscape mark the position of the spring. Just behind these trees is a dry waterfall. Cottonwood trees are a sign of water close by. The trees require more water to grow than most desert dwellers do. Cottonwoods are commonly found along streambeds, at spring sites, or along underground water seeps. The trees here at Cottonwood Spring use their long roots to tap into the spring's water, even if it is not available on the surface.

So rest and put your feet up under the shade of these cottonwoods, let the dog roll around in the gravel and relax. This is the end of the hike, but the area is open to investigation—venture out farther if you like. Return by walking back up the wash the way you came.

12. Crane's Nest Rapids

Round trip: 9.3 miles*
Elevation range: 655–2196 feet
Difficulty: Difficult
Hiking time: 5 hours
Best canine hiking seasons: Fall through spring
Under foot and paw: Gravel and rock
Regulations: Fee area. Dogs must be on a leash 6 feet long or less at all times. Waste must be removed and disposed of properly.
Map: USGS Ringbolt Rapids 7.5' quadrangle
Information: National Park Service, Alan Bible Visitor Center, (702) 293-8990 and (702) 293-8997, or *www.nps.gov/lame*
Water available: Colorado River

*4 miles with four-wheel-drive vehicle, with a hiking time of 2 hours

Getting there: This hike is located just past Hoover Dam on the Arizona side, along the Colorado River. To get there, take US Highway 95/93 south from Las Vegas. After passing through Henderson, US Highway 95 will split away from US Highway 93, 1 mile past the Railroad Pass Casino. Continue on US Highway 93 toward Boulder City. As you enter Boulder City, turn left at Buchanan/US Highway 93, which is the second stoplight. This road will continue from the light for 12 miles to Hoover Dam. Cross Hoover Dam to the Arizona side of the river. Turn right at mile marker 8. Park here if hiking the whole distance, or for the shorter hike, continue driving just over 3 miles and park where the gravel road turns to a hard rock surface.

If you and your dog loved the White Rock Canyon hike, you will find this hike just as spectacular and enjoyable. The general characteristics of both hikes are similar, but this canyon is a bit narrower and the canyon

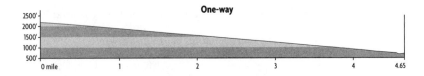

Opposite: Princess and Bailey cool off in the Colorado River.

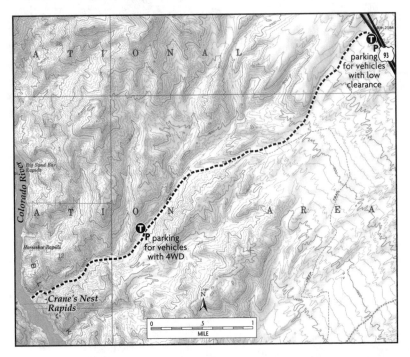

walls are more reddish-brown in color. Hikes like these are a pleasure to complete with dogs—they find it such a great treat to reach the Colorado River for a dip in the water! This hike is less known than White Rock Canyon, and usually has less traffic on the trail.

Travel down the dirt road as it moves to the southwest toward the river. There are interesting geologic formations along this first portion of the hike as well as many different plant species. After traveling just over 3 miles, the gravel road turns to a hard rock surface. (If you have driven in this far, park here.)

From here, continue down the wash. The canyon walls slowly narrow and become a deep rich brown and red in color. There are some areas where rock scrambling is necessary. Remember to check your pooch's paws regularly when scrambling. Be on the lookout for chipped nails and worn or cracked paw pads. Then the canyon walls open up and the fun begins. The Colorado River is stretched out before you with a lot of trees and bushes providing shade. On the south (left) side there is a spot with shaded access to the river. The water is shallow with a gravel bottom here and the current is minimal. After some rest and relaxation, return up the canyon to your vehicle—that is, if you can get your dog to leave!

13. Horsethief Canyon

Round trip: 11.2 miles*
Elevation range: 1553–3533 feet
Difficulty: Difficult without four-wheel drive, moderate (some scrambling) with four-wheel drive
Hiking time: 6 hours
Best canine hiking seasons: Fall through spring
Under foot and paw: Gravel and rock
Regulations: Fee area. Dogs must be on a leash 6 feet long or less at all times. Waste must be removed and disposed of properly.
Map: USGS Ringbolt Rapids and Hoover Dam 7.5' quadrangles
Information: National Park Service, Alan Bible Visitor Center, (702) 293-8990 and (702) 293-8997, or *www.nps.gov/lame*
Water available: Seasonal spring

*2.2 miles with four-wheel-drive vehicle, with a hiking time of 1.5 hours

Getting there: This hike is located just past Hoover Dam in Arizona, within Lake Mead National Recreation Area. To get there, take US Highway 95/93 south from Las Vegas. After passing through Henderson, US Highway 95 will split away from US Highway 93, 1 mile past the Railroad Pass Casino. Continue on US Highway 93 toward Boulder City. As you enter Boulder City, turn left at Buchanan/US Highway 93, which is the second stoplight. This road will continue from the light for 12 miles to Hoover Dam. Cross Hoover Dam to the Arizona side of the river. Just past mile marker 4, turn left into an unpaved parking area. Park here if hiking the entire distance or, for the shorter hike, continue driving another 4.5 miles (approximately) on the dirt road and park at the road's end.

Off the beaten path, Horsethief Canyon has a bit of everything. It is remote and offers a seasonal spring, wildlife, and some rock scrambling.

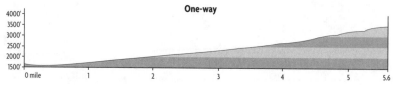

What more can a dog want? Depending on the season, the spring can be dry or, in winter and early spring, it may produce a small stream down the whole canyon. The rock scrambling is fun, but if it looks too difficult, there is always an easier alternate route to the side.

From the parking area off US Highway 93, walk or drive down the dirt road and cross a small bridge. Turn right just past the bridge onto a dirt road that leads up the wash. The road continues up the canyon in the wash itself. The wash bottom is gravelly and, in some cases, soft. Follow the large wash up toward the mountains. At the fork in the road, continue to the right. The road ends at the Horsethief Canyon trailhead. If you have driven in this far, park at the turnaround near a large dry waterfall.

For those who like to scramble, climb up the right side of the waterfall. This scramble is probably too much for all but the most athletic and scramble-happy dogs. For all others, hike up the hill to the left of the waterfall, then downslope to the wash above the falls. There is a small trail leading along this alternate route.

Follow the wash as it meanders up-canyon. A seasonal stream attracts wildlife to the area so be on the lookout for bighorn sheep, hawks, and quail. There are small side canyons along the way, but continue hiking up the main wash. In several areas there are cottonwood trees that provide shade for letting your dog take a break.

The wash ends in a box canyon with a waterfall and cottonwood tree. The story of this canyon is that long ago a man stole a horse in Kingman and rode across the desert to this area, chased by a band of men. He rode up the canyon and was boxed in at the waterfall area. He was captured and hung from a cottonwood tree. No one is sure if

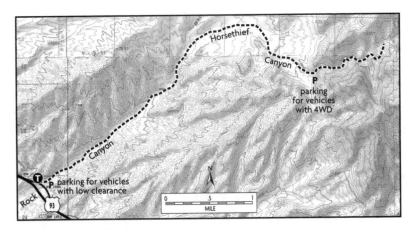

Entrance to Horsethief Canyon

the legend is true or not, but it does add some mystery to the outing. Return the way you came.

14. Liberty Bell Arch

Round trip: 4 miles
Elevation range: 1285–1647 feet
Difficulty: Moderate
Hiking time: 2.5 hours
Best canine hiking seasons: Fall through spring
Under foot and paw: Dirt, gravel, and some rock
Regulations: Fee area. Dogs must be on a leash 6 feet long or less at all times. Waste must be removed and disposed of properly.
Map: USGS Ringbolt Rapids 7.5' quadrangle
Information: National Park Service, Alan Bible Visitor Center, (702) 293-8990 and (702) 293-8997, or *www.nps.gov/lame*
Water available: No

Getting there: This hike is located just past Hoover Dam on the Arizona side, along the Colorado River. To get there, take US Highway 95/93

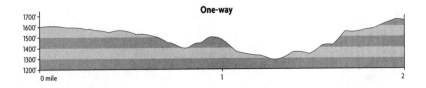

south from Las Vegas. After passing through Henderson, US Highway 95 will split away from US Highway 93, 1 mile past the Railroad Pass Casino. Continue on US Highway 93 toward Boulder City. As you enter Boulder City, turn left at Buchanan/US Highway 93, which is the second stoplight. This road will continue from the light for 12 miles to Hoover Dam. Cross over Hoover Dam to the Arizona side of the river. Park on the left in an unpaved parking area past the 3-mile marker but before the 4-mile marker. The parking area is where the hillside was cut back to make room for the road.

Do you ever wonder what is hidden out there in the desert, away from the roads and away from people? If so, this is a great hike for you and your dog. Along the Liberty Bell Arch trail you will pass an old mine site, a natural arch with an opening shaped like the Liberty Bell, and truly breathtaking views of the Colorado River, all of which feel like exciting discoveries along this unassuming trail.

This hike roughly parallels the White Rock Canyon hike to the north, but the similarities end there. While the White Rock Canyon hike runs through a shady canyon to the Colorado River, this hike is very exposed and leads to a high, spectacular overlook of the river. The trail can be a bit tough for the pooches because there is little to no shade available and the trail gains then loses elevation continuously (although the net difference is small). Time your trip for cool weather and bring plenty of water since there is none available on the trail. This trail is only recommended for fit dogs.

From the parking area, the first challenge is to cross the highway. Traffic in this area can be heavy and fast, so be cautious. After crossing the highway, walk west (right) along the road to the end of the hillside that has been cut out for the highway. At the end of the hill by the guardrails, there is an old roadway. Follow the old road for approximately 0.25 mile, until it starts to curve to the south. At this point, there will be a smaller trail leading off to the right. Take the smaller trail in a southwesterly direction. After a short distance it will fork; follow the fork to the left around a hillside.

After dropping down into a wash, the trail leads uphill toward the first discovery you and your dog will find—an old mine site. The mining area is quite obvious due to a very large wooden cable car that was once used to load rock into trucks that drove in on the dirt road. Around the time of World War II, magnesium was mined from this site. The mineshaft is just beyond the cable car. Carefully let your dog look around the mine site. As always, it is not recommended that you or your dog go into the mineshaft. The trail continues on a small path you will find just before the cable car, heading west.

This trail has a lot of elevation changes, with some twists and turns to keep your dog on its toes. Just after the mine site the trail leads briefly down into a wash, then back out of it. Your second discovery is only about 0.5 mile away. Just before the Liberty Bell Arch, the trail forks. Take the left (south) fork. The arch is high on the horizon to the west (right). You will actually have a better view of the arch after you pass it. Let your dog explore the rocky hillside just beyond the arch as you try to get a good

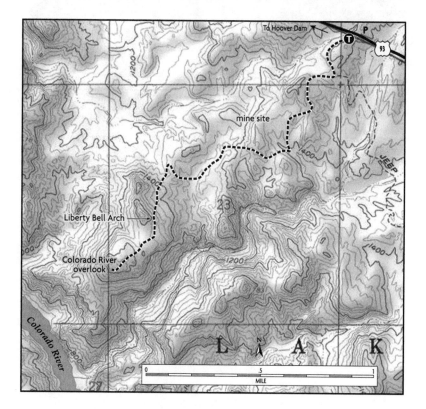

The Colorado River

picture of it. The opening that is shaped like the Liberty Bell is actually much bigger than it looks from the distance. Rumor has it that a small plane has flown through the opening.

After passing the Liberty Bell Arch, the trail begins to climb up a hillside toward the plateau that holds your third and last discovery. The trail is narrow here, and you and your dog will be climbing among rocks and boulders. As you follow the trail to the top of the plateau, watch for views of the Colorado River to the south. These views are little tidbits of what you are going to see at the top. The trail abruptly ends at the plateau with a 1000-foot drop below. Don't get too close to the edge, and remember—keep your dog on a leash! The river is visible both upstream and downstream. The view from this vantage point is so outstanding and awe-evoking, it is difficult to describe it fully. It really puts into perspective the awesome activity of the Colorado River, which slowly eroded this riverbed down from the elevation where you and your dog are standing to the river's current level far below. The bright blue water strongly contrasts with the dark gray and brown rock forming the surrounding cliffs on either side of the river. Carefully let your dog stand near the edge so the breeze can flap around its ears.

There is a cleared area on the plateau that makes a great lunch and resting spot for you and your pooch. After getting your fill of the views, return the way you came.

15. Lovell Canyon

Round trip: 6 miles*
Elevation range: 1700–2304 feet
Difficulty: Moderate
Hiking time: 3 hours
Best canine hiking seasons: Fall through spring
Under foot and paw: Sand, gravel, and some rock
Regulations: Fee area. Dogs must be on a leash 6 feet long or less at all times. Waste must be removed and disposed of properly.
Map: USGS Callville Bay 7.5' quadrangle
Information: National Park Service, Alan Bible Visitor Center, (702) 293-8990 and (702) 293-8997, or *www.nps.gov/lame*
Water available: No

*2 miles with four-wheel-drive vehicle, with a hiking time of 1 hour

Getting there: This hike is located near Callville Bay, within Lake Mead National Recreation Area. From Henderson, take Lake Mead Drive east. From the intersection with Boulder Highway, the fee station is 6.8 miles to the east. Just past the fee station, take a left onto Northshore Road. (Alternate directions: From the north side of the valley, take Lake Mead

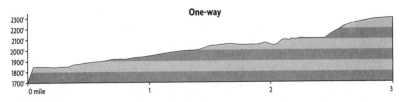

Boulevard east over Sunrise Mountain, past the fee station, and turn left onto Northshore Road.) Go north on Northshore Road and then make a left at mile marker 16. Park in the open unpaved area to the left if hiking the entire trail. If you have a high-clearance vehicle you can continue, parking about 2 miles farther up the canyon.

Nothing says "mysterious desert Southwest" better than a narrow slot canyon, and this is truly one of the best in this area. This hike is up the narrows of Lovell Wash, a tributary to the larger Callville Wash. The majority of the hike is open wash; then suddenly the canyon walls narrow and you walk into this amazing slot canyon. Your pooch will appreciate the change in scenery and the cooler temperatures. It will also have a blast weaving between the tight canyon walls!

Begin the hike down the dirt road. After 0.17 mile, the road will cross a wash. Just past the wash, the road will fork. Continue to the left (the road to the right leads up Callville Wash, Hike 10). After 0.5 mile from the parking area, there is a small road to the west (left) that leads up the wash. Stay on the main road instead of turning into the wash. After 1.2 miles there is a small open area with an informational sign about the Ore Car Mine and rock hobbyists. Continue on the road until just shy of 2 miles. For the shorter hike, drive your high-clearance vehicle to this point and then park in one of the several open areas just above a very large wash. Do not drive down to the wash.

Hike downhill to the large wash. Turn right and begin hiking up the wash. As you hike up this wide portion of the wash, you may see remnants of the Anniversary Mine on either side of the wash. There are several areas where the mineshafts are still open and accessible. View the shafts from a distance; old mineshafts can be hazardous. Keep your pet away from these mines as well. Reptiles such as rattlesnakes use areas like this to keep cool.

Two men, Lovell and Hartman from St. Thomas, discovered the borate deposit of this area in 1921. The West End Chemical Company purchased the mining interest and mined borate from 1921 to 1928. Competition from mines in California closed the mine seven years after it opened.

As you continue up the wash, the sides abruptly narrow to a slot canyon. The narrow canyon is several degrees cooler than the open desert and usually offers complete shade. After recent rains there can be standing water along the canyon bottom, but usually not in large amounts. If there is some water, though, by all means let your dog splash in it and play. As with any wash or canyon environment, do not attempt to hike in the rain or if rain is imminent, due to the risk of flash flooding. Parts of the canyon are very narrow; you will be able to touch both walls with outstretched arms. The canyon curves back

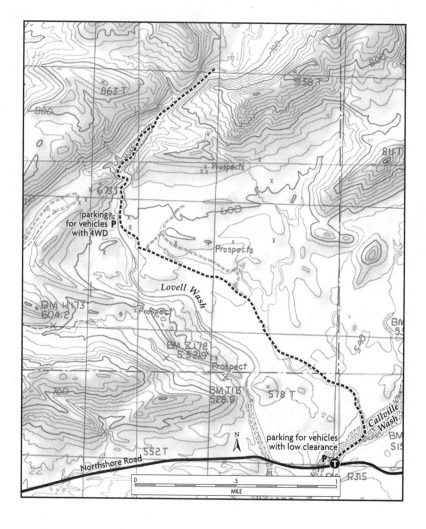

and forth and the walls stretch to the sky, making this an extraordinary experience. Your dog will love weaving around the corners and climbing up on the rocky outcrops between the tight canyon walls.

There are a few areas where rock scrambling is required to continue up the canyon. If your dog has short legs or doesn't like to rock scramble, you may have to lift it up here. As you reach the end of the canyon, the wash will widen out again. This is the end of the hike and a great picnic spot. Return the way you came through this incredible slot canyon and back to your vehicle.

Honey takes a break in Lovell Canyon.

16. Railroad Tunnel Trail

Round trip: 4.6 miles
Elevation range: 1560–1600 feet
Difficulty: Easy
Hiking time: 2.5 hours
Best canine hiking seasons: Fall through spring
Under foot and paw: Dirt and some fine gravel
Regulations: Fee area. Dogs must be on a leash 6 feet long or less at all times. Waste must be removed and disposed of properly.
Map: USGS Boulder Beach, 7.5' quadrangle
Information: National Park Service, Alan Bible Visitor Center, (702) 293-8990 and (702) 293-8997, or *www.nps.gov/lame*
Water available: No

Getting there: This hike is located just outside Boulder City, within Lake Mead National Recreation Area. To get there, take US Highway 95/93 south from Las Vegas. After passing through Henderson, US Highway 95 will split away from US 93 1 mile past the Railroad Pass Casino. Continue on US Highway 93 toward Boulder City. As you approach Boulder City, turn left at Buchanan/US Highway 93, which is the second stoplight. 4 miles after the stoplight, turn left onto Lakeshore Scenic Drive (follow signage to the Alan Bible Visitor Center). The Alan Bible Visitor Center will be on the left after a short distance. Continue past the visitor center 0.1 mile to a parking area on your right. Turn here and park in the parking area. This is the trailhead.

This trail is a defunct railroad bed with the tracks removed. It is wide and level with very little change in elevation. The easy terrain makes for great trail running with your dog, walking with a stroller, riding a bike, or taking a night hike. Best of all, this hike is great for our older dog friends that have a few years under their collar but still love to get out hiking.

The Railroad Tunnel Trail begins on the south side of the parking area

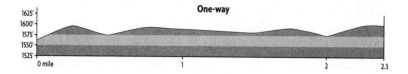

near an information kiosk. The trail winds quickly around to the left and passes through a chain-link gate that connects an opening cut out of a hillside. The gate is usually open but if it is closed, access can be gained immediately to the right of the gate.

In 1931, a contract was issued to a group of six major western firms to build the Hoover Dam construction railroad system, which was approximately 30 miles long. Five tunnels had to be blasted through the hillsides for this section of the railroad. All the tunnels, built for moving large equipment and huge penstock sections for the dam, are 25 feet in diameter and approximately 300 feet in length. The railroad was last used in 1961, and was dismantled shortly afterward and sold for scrap to Jucia Brothers. In 1984, the tunnels were nominated to the National Register of Historic Places. This trail is the only remaining section of the Hoover Dam railroad that is not highly disturbed or under water. As another note of historical interest, this trail was used in the motion picture *The Gauntlet*, starring Clint Eastwood. (It appears in a sequence where Eastwood, riding a motorcycle, is chased by an assassin in a helicopter.)

As you hike on the trail, Lake Mead is to your left. Since the trail is elevated well above the lake, you can see the entire Boulder Basin and the Boulder Islands. Be careful, though. The slopes on either side of the trail drop off quite dramatically at various points throughout the hike, so watch your dog if he is walking next to the edge.

The trail passes through all five tunnels. Several have been repaired from erosion or fire damage. The tunnels are often cool places for a nice

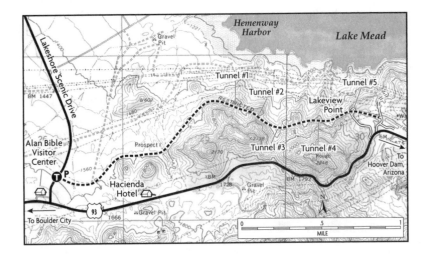

The Railroad Tunnel Trail is great for training.

respite and a bit of lunch if needed. If there is no one around, try and get your dog to bark in one of the tunnels. It sounds so much deeper and more ferocious than usual!

Just before the fourth tunnel, there is a small side trail that leads off to the left. This side path takes you to a nice viewpoint of the lake. The trail will lead you up a small hill that has loose rocks, so you and your dog will need to watch your footing. If you are hiking with an older dog, it is best to skip this side trail. If you are hiking with a hyper dog, he will enjoy the quick scramble.

As of this writing, the trail ends just after the fifth tunnel; farther passage is blocked by a gate near a series of government buildings. In the future, the intent is to have this trail link with the River Mountain Trail system. The trail will join another trail that leads to the top story of the Nevada parking structure at Hoover Dam. Just above the fifth tunnel is an overlook that can be accessed near Hoover Dam on US Highway 93. Don't be surprised if you have a few folks watching you hike along the trail (your dog may notice the people above before you do). Continue back the way you came.

17. Reverse Railroad to Knoll

Round trip: 1.8 miles
Elevation range: 1556–1675 feet
Difficulty: Easy
Hiking time: 1 hour
Best canine hiking seasons: Fall through spring
Under foot and paw: Sand, large rocks at knoll
Regulations: Fee area. Dogs must be on a leash 6 feet long or less at all times. Waste must be removed and disposed of properly.
Map: USGS Boulder Beach, 7.5' quadrangle
Information: National Park Service, Alan Bible Visitor Center, (702) 293-8990 and (702) 293-8997, or *www.nps.gov/lame*
Water available: No

Getting there: This hike is located just outside Boulder City, within Lake Mead National Recreation Area. To get there, take US Highway 95/93 south from Las Vegas. After passing through Henderson, US Highway 95 will split away from US 93 1 mile past the Railroad Pass Casino. Continue on US Highway 93 toward Boulder City. As you enter Boulder City, turn left at Buchanan/US Highway 93, which is the second stoplight. 4 miles after the stoplight, turn left onto Lakeshore Scenic Drive (follow signage

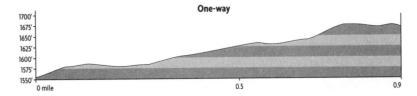

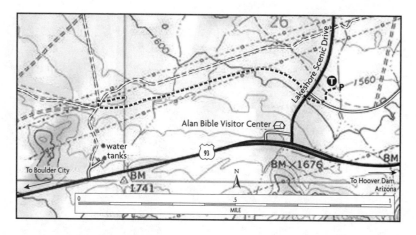

to the Alan Bible Visitor Center). The Alan Bible Visitor Center will be on the left after a short distance. Continue past the visitor center 0.1 mile to a parking area on your right. Turn here and park in the parking area.

This short trail offers a great stand-alone hike or a fun addition to the historic Railroad Tunnel Trail. The trail leads across the open desert with phenomenal views to the northeast of the Boulder Basin of Lake Mead. The hike described here ends by climbing up a small knoll to expansive views. Those interested in a longer hike can venture along the old railroad bed. The terrain is easy and flat for the majority of the hike; the only rocky portion is the knoll, so a variety of pooches will find this hike enjoyable.

If you have hiked the historic Railroad Tunnel Trail, you may have wondered where the path and tunnel going the opposite direction lead. This trail is the old railroad bed, following where it once made its way across the desert toward Boulder City. Begin the hike at the parking area, following the trail to the south. At the juncture in the trail, instead of going left to the Railroad Tunnel Trail, turn right and go through the tunnel underneath the road. This trail is level and well groomed, making it accessible for bicycles and jogging strollers as well. This hike would also be good for an older dog, or a dog that doesn't do well in varied terrain. Just skip the knoll for these pets.

The trail leads in a straight line across the desert toward the River Mountains. The trail described here is part of the planned River Mountains Loop Trail System, a 35-mile trail that will go from Boulder City through the Lake Mead National Recreation Area into Henderson and then back around to Boulder City. This trail system is currently under

Boulder Basin and the surrounding mountains

construction, with some areas completed and some just in the planning stages.

While hiking on this trail, you'll notice an area of dense mesquite on the south (left) side of the trail. Many animals use dense brush to make their homes or to rest in during the heat of the day. Your dog may perk up in this area as it senses the creatures hiding out here. Continue along the trail until you come to a small knoll on the north (right) side of the trail. (If you cross a large dirt road you have gone too far.) Walk past the knoll and hike up the far side. There is a primitive trail up this portion, leading to the top of the knoll. If your pet is not good on this type of terrain, skip the knoll; there are still wonderful views from the main trail.

If you have climbed the knoll, sit down and relax a minute and soak up the scenery. The islands in view are the Boulder Islands, and this whole area of the lake is called the Boulder Basin. After you have completed your sightseeing, return the way you came.

18. River Mountain Trail

Round trip: 5.1 miles
Elevation range: 2417–3429 feet
Difficulty: Moderate
Hiking time: 3 hours
Best canine hiking seasons: Fall through spring
Under foot and paw: Dirt
Regulations: Fee area. Dogs must be on a leash 6 feet long or less
    at all times. Waste must be removed and disposed of properly.
Map: USGS Boulder City 7.5' quadrangle
Information: National Park Service, Alan Bible Visitor Center,
    (702) 293-8990 and (702) 293-8997, or *www.nps.gov/lame*
Water available: No

Getting there: This hike is located in Boulder City. To get there, take US
Highway 95/93 south from Las Vegas. After passing through Henderson,
US Highway 95 will split away from US 93 1 mile past the Railroad Pass
Casino. Continue on US Highway 93 toward Boulder City. As you enter
Boulder City, turn left at Buchanan/US Highway 93, which is the second
stoplight. Turn left 0.6 mile from the stoplight into the parking area
after crossing over a small bridge and culvert. The trail begins behind
the information board.

Lizards and tortoises and birds, oh my! This trail has a host of wildlife
inhabiting the lower portions of the trail. Your dog will enjoy the smells
and sights of ground squirrels, lizards, and an occasional desert tortoise.
As the hike begins to switchback, you will realize why this hike is designated "moderate." The climb is worthwhile, though, because the views
from the top are breathtaking. You can sit and look at Lake Mead, then
turn around and see Las Vegas with Mount Charleston in the background.
Be aware that this trail is also used by mountain bikers, so if your dog

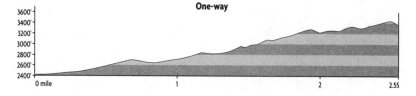

does not like bikes speeding by, this may not be the best trail for your day's adventure.

Before beginning the hike, check the information kiosk for pamphlets about the trail. The National Park Service, Boulder City, and the University of Nevada have collaborated and put together an informative self-guided tour pamphlet about the area's geology and other features. Pamphlets are also available at the Alan Bible Visitor Center.

The hike begins behind the kiosk and proceeds along the metal railing on the left side of the flood channel. The trail starts on the edge of a

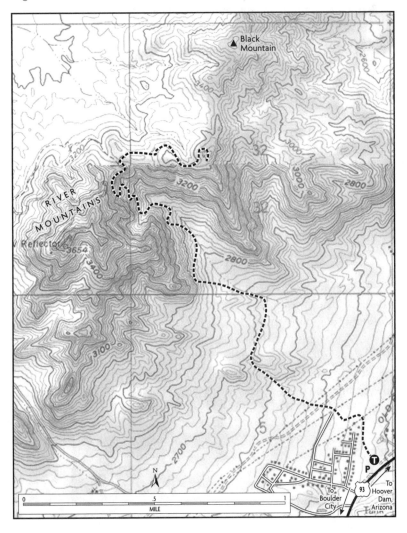

Views are phenomenal from the top of Black Mountain overlook.

residential community, then moves out onto public land. This portion of the hike is in open desert, gradually increasing in elevation. At times the trail crosses hilltops, other times it runs along the wash bottom. Throughout the hike, the trail is well maintained and easily identified, but several other trails do cross the main trail in the open desert area. Stay on the larger trail, lined on either side with rocks.

Your dog will be happy to know that it is common to see wildlife on this trail, especially in the cooler morning or evening hours. Do not be surprised if you have to share the trail with a desert tortoise along the way. Keep your pet in control, there's no chasing lizards or ground squirrels here!

One of the most interesting facts about this trail is how long it has been in existence. It was built by the Civilian Conservation Corps (CCC) over sixty-six years ago in 1937–1938. The CCC was active in Nevada during that time. It built beaches at Lake Mead, cabins at Valley of Fire State Park, and roads in the Mount Charleston area, just to name a few of its projects.

This trail is now part of the Bootleg Canyon Trail system, which has many trails for hikers and has really begun to get a name for its mountain-biking trails. The name Bootleg Canyon comes from the time when Boulder City was a federal city primarily for construction workers building Boulder Dam. The city was "dry," with alcoholic beverages banned within the city limits, and stills were hidden up in the canyons of this mountain system to supply black-market alcohol for the residents who wanted it. Remember while you are hiking here that bikes have the right of way; step aside and let the bikers pass. Many mountain bikers use bells to warn of their approach (see "Good Canine Trail Etiquette" in Part I).

When nearing the mountains, the trail begins to switchback, gaining elevation. This is the area where you and you pooch will have to work the hardest. After 2 miles from the trailhead, the trail reaches a saddle and forks. Continue to the east (right) to the Black Mountain overlook. To the west (left) is Red Mountain. Another trail will fork off to the left down the hillside; continue on the trail moving gradually to the right. After 0.55 mile from the fork, the trail ends at the mountaintop. At the top, there are benches and information plaques describing the area.

From the overlook, the 360-degree view is astounding. To the east and northeast you can see the Boulder Basin in Lake Mead, with views into Arizona. To the south and southeast is Boulder City. To the west and northwest is the Las Vegas Valley, with Mount Charleston in the distance. After a little sightseeing, some rest, and possibly a few dog biscuits, return the way you came.

19. River Mountains Loop Trail—Segment 17

Round trip: 4.94 miles
Elevation range: 1667–1314 feet
Difficulty: Moderately easy
Hiking time: 2 hours
Best canine hiking seasons: Fall through spring
Under foot and paw: Gravel road
Regulations: Fee area. Dogs must be on a leash 6 feet long or less at all times. Waste must be removed and disposed of properly.
Map: USGS Henderson and Boulder Beach 7.5' quadrangles
Information: National Park Service, Alan Bible Visitor Center, (702) 293-8990 and (702) 293-8997, or *www.nps.gov/lame*. Also try the River Mountains Loop Trail website, *www.rivermountainstrail.org*
Water available: No

Getting there: This hike is located near the entrance of Lake Mead National Recreation Area along Lake Mead Drive. From Henderson, take

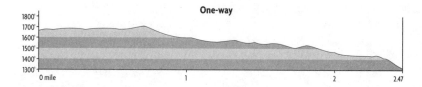

Lake Mead Drive east. From the intersection with Boulder Highway, the fee station is 6.8 miles to the east. Lake Mead Drive turns into Lakeshore Scenic Drive as you enter the recreation area. Approximately 0.1 mile before the fee station, on the south (right) side of the road, is Loren Williams Parkway. Turn right onto the paved Parkway. The road quickly turns into a dirt road. Park your vehicle in the disturbed area on the right side of the road.

The River Mountains Loop Trail is a system of twenty-two trails that link together to form a 35-mile loop around the River Mountains. At the time of this writing, this is a new project being completed by Lake Mead National Recreation Area, the city of Boulder City, and city of Henderson. Segment 17 of this trail system offers nice views of Lake Mead and the mountains. The trail follows the alignment of the BMI (Basic Management, Inc.) pipeline from Lake Mead to the BMI facilities in Henderson. Since the trail is also used for maintenance of the pipeline, it is a wide-graded path. This is a great trail for dogs that can't rock scramble or are beginning their fitness training, or for trail running.

Begin your hike by heading east toward Lake Mead. You will immediately encounter a locked gate, which is easy to pass around or under. The gate is meant to block vehicles, not hikers. Just past the gate is a large disturbed area. Just before the disturbed area, the dirt road bends to the south (right). Do not follow the bend. Instead, continue walking straight, staying to the north (left) side of the dirt piles. This is the trickiest part of the trail, because it seems like you should be going right, not straight. There is often a lot of trash in this area. Once you get past the disturbed area, the trail follows a nice graded dirt roadway toward the lake. Along the way are several small hills to ascend and descend as you admire the views of Lake Mead and the natural desert around you.

Segment 17 is a moderately easy trail and very underutilized. For this reason, it is a great route for dogs and dog owners who are just starting to hike together. If you are looking for a place to practice trail etiquette commands with your dog, this is it. There are more stimuli along the

Sida gets a refreshing drink.

hike than at your house, making it a natural step up from training at home or at your local park. Segment 17 can also be used as a training hike to get your dog in better shape for longer hikes. The distance on this hike is moderate and there are several small hills to climb. If you like trail running with your dog, Segment 17 is a good choice because there are not many rocks along the trail. Also, the trail is about 10 feet wide so you and your pup don't have to squeeze between bushes or pointy yucca plants.

Segment 17 ends when the trail intersects the old Lakeshore Scenic Drive, which is just west of the current road. If you would like to continue your hike, the old paved, abandoned road serves as Segment 18 of the River Mountains Loop system. If not, follow your footsteps back to your car. On the return trip there are beautiful views of the River Mountains.

Hiking tip: If you are interested in a longer hike or a one-way hike, convince a friend to go with you. Park one car by the fish hatchery described in Segment 18 (Hike 20), and one car at the beginning of this trail. Hike Segment 17 to Segment 18. Continue on Segment 18 to the fish hatchery, then drive back and get the car you left at the trailhead for Segment 17. Together, these two segments make a nice hike about 6 miles long. By starting with Segment 17, most of the hike is downhill.

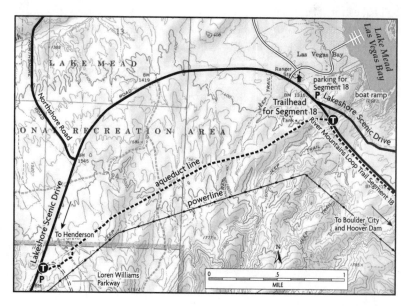

20. River Mountains Loop Trail—Segment 18

Round trip: 7.14 miles
Elevation range: 1331–1522 feet
Difficulty: Moderate
Hiking time: 2.5–3.5 hours
Best canine hiking seasons: Fall through spring
Under foot and paw: Paved road
Regulations: Fee area. Dogs must be on a leash 6 feet long or less at all times. Waste must be removed and disposed of properly.
Map: USGS Boulder Beach 7.5' quadrangle
Information: National Park Service, Alan Bible Visitor Center, (702) 293-8990 and (702) 293-8997, or *www.nps.gov/lame*. Also try the River Mountains Loop Trail website, *www.rivermountainstrail.org*
Water available: No

Getting there: This hike is located near the Las Vegas Bay within the Lake Mead National Recreation Area. From Henderson, take Lake Mead Drive east. From the intersection with Boulder Highway, the fee station is 6.8 miles to the east. From the fee station, continue driving straight on Lakeshore Scenic Drive. Lakeshore Scenic Drive will turn to the right, heading south. Approximately 2.3 miles past the fee station is the Las Vegas Bay Scenic Overlook. Park your car in the parking lot and carefully lead your dog across the road to the south side of Lakeshore Scenic Drive. Directly across from the parking lot is a road with a gate. This is the trailhead. Walk around the gate and start hiking south.

Alternately, you can approach this trail from the south and park at the opposite end, near a fish hatchery. Between mile markers 5 and 6 on Lakeshore Scenic Drive is a fish hatchery. To get to the fish hatchery from the Las Vegas Bay Scenic Overlook, continue driving south on Lakeshore

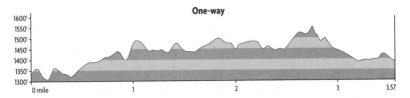

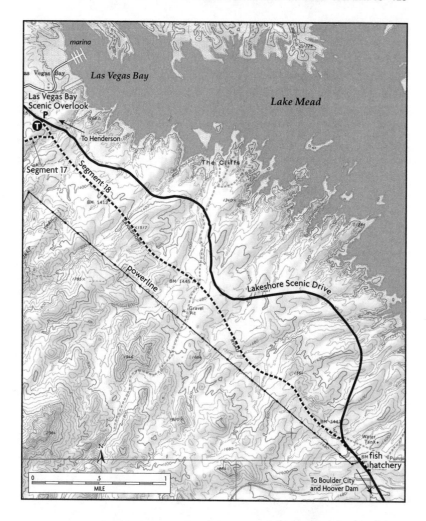

Scenic Drive. Turn left off Lakeshore Scenic Drive at the fish hatchery and park on the left side of the road near, but not blocking, the mailboxes. If you bring a friend to hike with you, you can park one car at the fish hatchery, and one at the Las Vegas Bay Scenic Overlook, giving you a one-way hike of 3.57 miles. If you would like to hike farther, you can combine this hike with the River Mountains Loop Trail Segment 17 to make an approximately 6-mile hike, described under Hike 19.

Do you have a senior dog that is no longer agile or sharp-eyed enough to climb rocks? Or maybe you enjoy running with your dog? This hike is great in either case because it is entirely on an old, paved, abandoned road. The trail, following the old alignment of the Lakeshore Scenic Drive, offers great views of Lake Mead as well as some narrow side canyons with interesting rock features. If your dog is not physically able to hike on a rocky trail, this trail will enable you and your four-legged friend to get out and enjoy the lake while still getting some exercise.

From the gate, walk south on the old Lakeshore Scenic Drive. This is a roadway that has been closed off to all motorized vehicles and horses. Since this is a paved trail, it is very easy to follow. For slightly more than 3.5 miles, the trail heads south while winding through the desert. This is a very enjoyable hike because you really do not have to worry about anything. Other than crossing the road to get to and from the trail to your car, there are no major hazards. While winding through the desert, you will have the opportunity to enjoy beautiful views of the lake and the canyons the road traverses. Your dog will enjoy the wind blowing by his ears. Quite frequently the abandoned roadway that serves as your trail will be littered with bighorn sheep scat (small, dark pellets, usually oblong and slightly pointed at one end). It may be because the roadway is an easy transportation corridor, but for whatever reason, bighorn sheep obviously use this area. Since bighorn are very elusive animals, there is a good chance they will see you and flee before you see them.

Paved trail with great views of Lake Mead

If you and your dog are fortunate enough to see them, remember that the sheep see your dog as a predator. So keep your distance. Even if you don't see a bighorn sheep, just their scent along the trail will keep your dog's tail wagging.

After about 3.5 miles, the trail will intersect the new Lakeshore Scenic Drive. If you parked at the Las Vegas Bay Scenic Overlook, turn around and retrace your path back to the car. Your return trip will be slightly uphill. If you parked at the south end of the trail, the fish hatchery will be around the corner from where the two roads meet. Continue walking on the side of the road to just before the bend in the road. The shoulder is wide here, so it is fairly safe for you and your dog. When you have a good vantage point of both directions of traffic along Lakeshore Scenic Drive, carefully lead your dog to the east side of the road. Continue walking south a very short distance to the mailboxes for the fish hatchery, and your car.

21. Sunset View

Round trip: 0.6 mile to point, various beyond this area
Elevation range: 1158–1240 feet
Difficulty: Easy
Hiking time: 0.5 hour
Best canine hiking seasons: All year
Under foot and paw: Dirt and rock
Regulations: Fee area. Dogs must be on a leash 6 feet long or less
　　at all times. Waste must be removed and disposed of properly.
Map: USGS Boulder Beach 7.5' quadrangle
Information: National Park Service, Alan Bible Visitor Center,
　　(702) 293-8990 and (702) 293-8997, or *www.nps.gov/lame*
Water available: Lake Mead

Getting there: This hike is located a short distance south of the Las Vegas Bay within the Lake Mead National Recreation Area. From Henderson, take Lake Mead Drive east. From the intersection with Boulder Highway,

the fee station is 6.8 miles to the east. Continue on Lake Mead as it turns into Lakeshore Scenic Drive. The Sunset View overlook and parking area are clearly marked 5.5 miles past the fee station.

It's hot out. You don't have much time, but the dogs are itching to go outside and get some exercise. This is the perfect stroll for an after-work or quick weekend activity—and it includes swimming! Sunset Point, on the west side of Boulder Basin at Lake Mead, has striking views of the entire basin, day or night. On a full moon night the water shimmers in the light, with the dark islands of the basin looking beautifully serene. The walk is short and the swimming great, but keep an eye out for trash along the trail that might be hazardous to your dog.

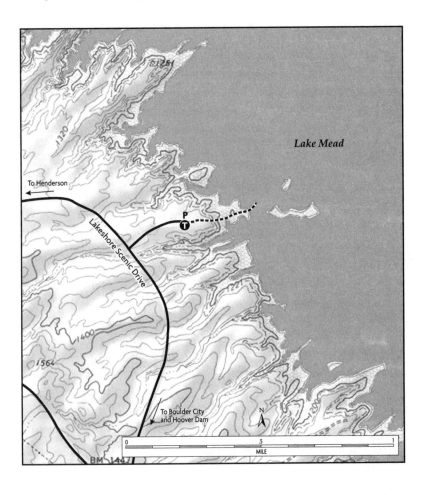

The Sunset View hike is all about getting wet at Lake Mead.

From the parking area, look east. The hike goes to the point jutting out into the water due east. To get there, hike down the slope on the north side of the parking area toward the water. Continue on a narrow trail out to the point. Depending on wind direction, hike to the north or south side of the point, which ever is best protected, and jump in! There are several little coves, and more hills and points to explore in the area to the north and south. Watch for litter such as broken glass or fishing line. This area is much-used by people and dogs alike.

Lake Mead water temperatures are commonly reported on local news reports, so it might be worth checking beforehand. August usually has the highest water temperatures, commonly in the low to mid 80s in the sheltered coves. Although it might be too hot during the day in August, a nice full moon evening of swimming can be quite wonderful.

Swimming is great exercise for both humans and dogs. If your dog does not enjoy the water or has not been exposed to swimming previously, take it slow. Forcing a dog to swim may scare it away from the experience for its lifetime. Walk into the water a few feet and encourage your pooch to follow you, giving lavish praise or a treat for each step taken into the water. Continue the process until the dog is in deep enough water to swim. Some dogs may never become active swimmers, deciding instead to be waders, enjoying the cool water while keeping all four paws firmly on solid ground. Either way, it feels great on a hot summer day! Once you have finished having fun, return to your vehicle the way you came.

"The most affectionate creature in the world is a wet dog."

—*Ambrose Bierce* (Collected Works, 1909–1912,
Gordian Press, 1966)

22. Teddy Bear Cholla Forest

Round trip: 4.5 miles*
Elevation range: 1580–2490 feet
Difficulty: Moderate
Hiking time: 2.5–3.5 hours
Best canine hiking seasons: Fall through spring
Under foot and paw: Dirt road
Regulations: Fee area. Dogs must be on a leash 6 feet long or less
　　at all times. Waste must be removed and disposed of properly.
Map: USGS Boulder Beach 7.5' quadrangle
Information: National Park Service, Alan Bible Visitor Center,
　　(702) 293-8990 and (702) 293-8997, or *www.nps.gov/lame*
Water available: No

*0.6 mile with a high-clearance vehicle, hiking time 0.5 hour

Getting there: This hike is located just outside Boulder City, within Lake Mead National Recreation Area. To get there, take US Highway 95/93 south from Las Vegas. After passing through Henderson, US Highway 95 will split away from US 93 1 mile past the Railroad Pass Casino. Continue on US Highway 93 toward Boulder City. As you approach Boulder City,

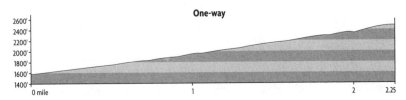

turn left at Buchanan/US Highway 93, which is the second stoplight. After 4 miles from the stoplight, turn left onto Approved Route 76 (AR 76), which is a dirt road. The easiest way to spot the turn-off is to look for a water tank and pumping station. (If you miss the dirt road, there is a viewing area about 0.1 mile past the dirt road on the left side of the road. Turn around here, or go a little farther east to the Alan Bible Visitor Center and turn around.) From AR 76, drive 0.8 mile to Approved Route 77 (AR 77), which will be to the left. Park your car off to the side of the road. If you are interested in a very short hike of less than a mile, high-clearance vehicles can drive about 2 miles farther in on the dirt road and park by the powerline pole marked "57." The hike follows AR 77 toward the mountains to the east.

Don't worry. Despite the name, your dog will not be navigating through cacti on this hike. This trail is a great adventure if you like to go jogging with your four-legged friend. The trail follows a dirt road to a secret forest of teddy bear cholla cacti. The cacti are off to the side of the road, hidden until you turn a corner just before you reach them: an impressive sight that you don't often see. If for some reason a cactus spine does become attached to you or your dog on this hike (or any other desert hike), use sticks or a wide-toothed comb to remove it. If it is deeply imbedded, use scissors to remove the main piece, and go after the remaining spines with pliers. As long as your dog is under control, this should not be an issue since the cacti are off the dirt road.

From the intersection of AR 76 and AR 77, begin hiking along AR 77 west to the mountains, following the powerline route. The vegetation along the road mainly consists of creosote bush, brittlebush, and white bursage, with an occasional barrel cactus or beavertail cactus. During springtime there are many wildflowers in the area including the globe mallow, a shrub-size plant with many small orange flowers, and lupine, a smaller plant with pretty purple flowers. There are few people in this area, so take the time to let your dog stop and smell the flowers. Smell them for yourself as well. Since few people know about the hidden forest, no one will see you! After about 1.5 miles, a few teddy bear cholla start growing along the side of the road.

If you take your dog trail running, this is a good trail for it. In some parts it is rockier than others, but for the most part it will make for a good run. While you are walking or jogging, though, look for the power pole that is marked "57," about 2 miles into the hike. Just beyond pole 57 there is a dirt road leading to the left, marked for "Authorized Vehicles Only." Follow this dirt road around the corner and, after 0.3 mile, you will be standing next to an impressive stand of teddy bear cholla.

Teddy bear cholla are said to look like the fuzzy arms and legs of a teddy bear. As you get closer, you will realize that this is as far from the truth as

Rick and his dog Bear inspect a forest of cacti.

it gets. The cactus actually has a tree-like stem with dense, straw-colored spines. Their yellow-to-green flowers bloom between February and May. The spines are hooked so they can catch easily into animals' skin (including your dog's, if it is not under control and runs into the forest). The joints that the spines are connected to detach easily from the mother plant; when they fall to the ground, a new cactus plant will grow. A few animals are known to take advantage of the sharp, densely growing spines. Pack rats will drag the spiny joints to their home and position them so predators cannot get in. The cactus wren, surprisingly enough, creates a nest in the cactus, because its spines keep predators away from her young.

After you are done admiring the stand of cactus, follow your footsteps to get back to your car. The return trip is very enjoyable, as it is slightly downhill with expansive views of Lake Mead.

23. White Rock Canyon to Colorado River

Round trip: 5 miles
Elevation range: 655–1543 feet
Difficulty: Moderate
Hiking time: 3 hours
Best canine hiking seasons: Fall through spring
Under foot and paw: Gravel and rock
Regulations: Fee area. Dogs must be on a leash 6 feet long or less at all times. Waste must be removed and disposed of properly.
Map: USGS Ringbolt Rapids 7.5' quadrangle
Information: National Park Service, Alan Bible Visitor Center, (702) 293-8990 and (702) 293-8997, *www.nps.gov/lame*
Water available: Colorado River

Getting there: This hike is located just past Hoover Dam on the Arizona side, along the Colorado River. To get there, take US 95/93 south from Las Vegas toward Boulder City. After passing through Henderson, US 95 will split away from US 93, 1 mile past the Railroad Pass Casino. Continue on US 93 toward Boulder City. As you approach Boulder City, turn left at the second stoplight onto Buchanan/US 93. This road will continue from the light for 12 miles to Hoover Dam. Cross Hoover Dam to the Arizona side of the river. Between mile markers 4 and 5 there is a short dirt road

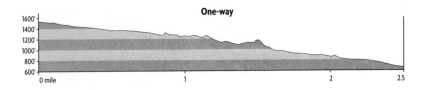

on the right, with a parking area at the end of it. The trail begins from the parking area. As with any other parking area, pay close attention to your dog—you are near a busy highway!

This trail is a treat for the owner and for the dog. From the trailhead you see a lot of open desert, but then the trail takes you back to a cool shaded canyon and down to the Colorado River, where dogs can swim and enjoy the water.

The trailhead is a clearly marked sign at the edge of the parking area. The beginning of the trail leads in a westerly direction, parallel to a large wash on the right. After about 0.5 mile the trail drops down into the wash. The remainder of the hike is in the wash as it winds down to the Colorado River. Walking in the sand may give you more of a workout than you expected, especially on your return trip since it is slightly uphill. Make sure you and your dog are in good shape for this hike.

For approximately 1 mile, the wash is wide and open. Then the wash moves into a tight, weaving canyon. At this point, the canyon walls are high, and temperatures are cooler due to the walls' shading effect. Throughout the hike, the canyon widens and narrows repeatedly, and in turn the wash widens back and forth, creating shaded areas for you and you pooch to relax in as you enjoy the impressive rock walls.

The Colorado River is at the end of the wash. It is well worth your effort to continue to the river for the recreational opportunities that await your dog. As you near the river, the canyon walls open up to a beach area. This is a wonderful area to stop and picnic and let the dogs enjoy the water. The Hoover Dam is a short distance up the river, to your right. The water flowing is from the bottom portion of Lake Mead, so it is very cool and refreshing. On the downstream side of the beach is a small shallow cove with a slower current—a great place for dogs to swim.

After splashing in the river, we recommend following your footprints back toward the car. The trail does continue to the left, following the river

Opposite: Swimming is an added treat to an already fun hike.

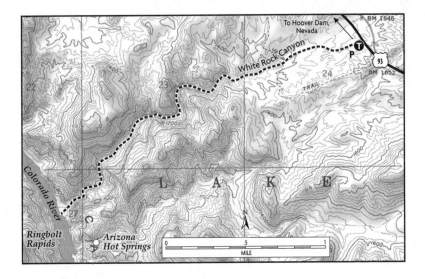

south, toward a popular hot spring area (Arizona Hot Springs). While this is a fun recreational area, it is not a good place to visit with your dog. To get to the springs there is a tall ladder, approximately 20 feet tall, that you must climb. These springs also contain an amoeba called *Naegleria fowleri,* which has been known to cause serious health problems for people and animals when it enters the body.

RED ROCK CANYON NATIONAL CONSERVATION AREA

Red Rock Canyon National Conservation Area (NCA) is one of the greatest outdoor areas around Las Vegas. The area is internationally known by outdoors enthusiasts and geologists alike for its sandstone and limestone cliffs. In 1967, 10,000 acres were set aside to create the Red Rock Canyon Recreation Lands. In 1990, this area was expanded to 83,100 acres and renamed the Red Rock Canyon National Conservation Area. Since then, the area has more than doubled to its current size of 197,000 acres.

Red Rock Canyon NCA hosts a variety of recreational activities such as hiking, rock climbing, mountain biking, and horseback riding. Unlike the Vegas valley floor, Red Rock is at a higher elevation, and has a lusher environment with typically twice the rainfall of the valley. The Red Rock Canyon area, part of the Spring Mountains Range, has more springs than any other part of the desert in this region, providing water for a variety of wildlife. Cool breezes from the higher elevations of the Mount Charleston area flow down the narrow canyons of the Red Rock area, creating unique microclimates: habitat for plant and animal species not found elsewhere in this region, such as ponderosa pines.

A plethora of animal species live in Red Rock Canyon, including bighorn sheep, wild burros, the desert tortoise, and coyotes. More than

600 plant species make this area their home, with some endemic species that grow nowhere else in the world, such as the rough angelica from the carrot family and the Red Rock Canyon aster from the sunflower family. This area is also known for its unique geological formations and abundance of cultural resource sites.

One of the best things about Red Rock is that it is very accessible, almost in the city now that Las Vegas has grown to the edges of the valley. For those living on Las Vegas's west side, hiking in this area is quite convenient, and many of the hikes can be completed after work.

Please note: Portions of Red Rock Canyon NCA require a fee for entrance, including the Red Rock Canyon Scenic Drive. The entrance fee for a car is $5.00, and an annual pass can be purchased for $20.00.

24. Calico Tanks

Round trip: 2.4 miles
Elevation range: 4305–4744 feet
Difficulty: Moderate
Hiking time: 1.5 hours
Best canine hiking seasons: Fall through spring
Under foot and paw: Sand and sandstone rock
Regulations: Fee area. Dogs must be on a leash 6 feet long or less. Waste, including but not limited to dog waste, must be removed and disposed of properly.
Map: USGS La Madre Mountain 7.5' quadrangle
Information: Bureau of Land Management, Red Rock Canyon National Conservation Area, (702) 515-5350, or *www.redrockcanyon.blm.gov*
Water available: In rainy seasons, water in natural sandstone depressions

Getting there: This hike is located off the Red Rock Canyon Scenic Drive in the Red Rock Canyon National Conservation Area (NCA). From the northern part of the Las Vegas Valley, take Charleston Boulevard west toward the Spring Mountains. The entrance to the Red Rock Canyon Scenic Drive is on the north (right) side of the road, approximately 5 miles past the intersection of Charleston Boulevard and State Highway 215 (Las Vegas Beltway). (Alternate directions: From the southern part of the Las Vegas Valley, take Interstate 15 to the Nevada Highway 160 exit

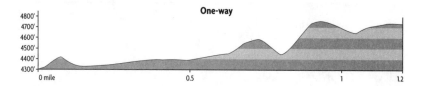

One-way

4800'
4700'
4600'
4500'
4400'
4300'

0 mile   0.5   1   1.2

(Blue Diamond Road). Head west on Highway 160 for 10 miles, then turn right onto Nevada Highway 159. After 10 miles, turn left into the Red Rock Canyon NCA.) Enter the fee area and take the Red Rock Canyon Scenic Drive just over 2.5 miles to the Sandstone Quarry parking lot. The trailhead is at the north end of the parking lot.

This trail is just fun, fun, fun. It is in a beautiful sandstone area with a lot of twists, a little bit of scrambling, and an enjoyable amount of diversity in the plant life that will keep your dog wagging its tail for more. Not a section of this hike can be considered boring. The trail moves between two sandstone ridges, up to a large *tinaja* (Spanish for tank), or a natural depression in the sandstone, that typically has water in it. This trail is great for almost any healthy, fit dog that can handle a moderate amount of light rock scrambling.

The trail begins at the parking area near the kiosk and restrooms. From here, lead your dog downhill a short distance to a cleared area about half the size of a basketball court. You and your dog are standing in an old sandstone quarry. Sandstone is the rock you see to your right. On the north side of the cleared area are several large, square pieces of rock left behind from the quarry operation. The rock was mined from this area and sent to Las Vegas, San Francisco, and Los Angeles for stonework in houses. Some of the rocks that were cut out of the hillside here weighed up to ten tons! Let your dog climb up on the sandstone and then down into the quarry area. This is probably the only mine site in southern Nevada that is safe to explore.

Once done exploring the sandstone quarry, continue down the trail across a wash. There is a sign showing the way and the trail is very well defined, so you and your puppy dog should not have a hard time following it. If for some reason you end up walking north in the wash, fear not: the wash crosses paths with the trail again. About 0.25 mile in on the trail, you and your dog will notice a large agave roasting pit on the left. Make sure to keep your dog back, since this is a cultural resource left behind by early Native Americans. Just past the roasting pit is another trail sign showing that the Calico Tanks trail continues to the right, and

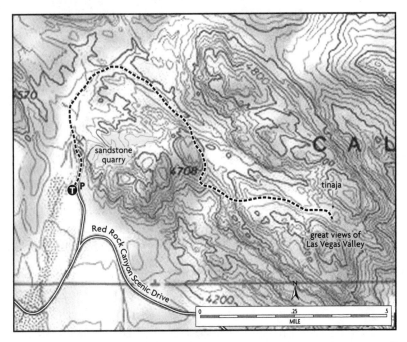

Turtlehead to the left. Turtlehead is the tall limestone outcrop just off to your left. While it is a great hike for humans, the loose terrain is not the best for doggies.

From the sign, the trail curves around to the east (right) and the path weaves through a small patch of trees and bushes. This is another exciting part of the trail, so let your dog sniff around. There is also a small patch of extremely soft sand in this area. Anybody up for a good roll in the sand? After the soft sand, the trail continues up between the Calico Hills. The rest of the trail is slightly uphill, and there is a bit of rock scrambling. At one point there is even a set of sandstone steps created to help you climb to the upper level. This area should not be too difficult for any dog in decent shape. Depending on the time of year and if there has been a recent rainstorm, there may be some fun puddles created when the water catches in the sandstone depressions. If your dog likes splashing, get your fill of it here because it is not recommended at the watering hole at the end of the trail. While you are hiking up through this area, also keep your eye out for rock climbers. In all likelihood, your dog may spot them first. There are several climbing routes up on the left

Opposite: The sandstone hillsides make for great scrambling.

side of the trail. Aside from seeing or hearing the climbers, you may run across a dog wandering around the area. Sometimes rock climbers will take their dogs with them and leave them at the base of the climb. It is always bothersome to see a dog wander around without an apparent owner, but if you are in that situation, just walk over to the base of the climbers' rock and yell up at them.

As the trail reaches the summit, the path becomes a bit narrower and steeper. The trail presses against the left hillside and leads you to a large *tinaja*. At various points of the year the *tinaja* may have anywhere from a few feet of water in it to none. If there is water in the *tinaja*, please just let your dog admire from a distance. This is a primary water source for the animals that live in the area, including a herd of bighorn sheep that are often seen on the backside of the Calico Hills.

If you and your dog have good balance, you can carefully navigate around the south side of the *tinaja* to the rocks on the east side of the area. There is a great view of Las Vegas from here. Once you are done exploring the area, guide your dog back through the hills to your car.

25. First Creek

Round trip: 2 miles
Elevation range: 3638–3838 feet
Difficulty: Easy
Hiking time: 1 hour
Best canine hiking seasons: Fall through spring
Under foot and paw: Dirt with some rocks
Regulations: Dogs must be on a leash 6 feet long or less. Waste, including but not limited to dog waste, must be removed and disposed of properly.
Map: USGS Blue Diamond 7.5' quadrangle
Information: Bureau of Land Management, Red Rock Canyon National Conservation Area, (702) 515-5350, or *www.redrockcanyon.blm.gov*
Water available: Seasonal creek

Getting there: This hike is located in the Red Rock Canyon National Conservation Area (NCA), but it is not accessed from the Red Rock Canyon Scenic Drive. From the northern part of the valley take I 215 to Charleston Boulevard. Head west for 5 miles to the entrance for Red

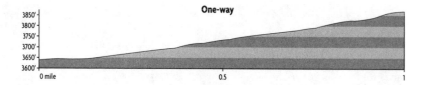

Rock Canyon NCA. Pass the entrance and drive 4.3 miles to the First Creek parking lot on the right side of the road. (Alternate directions: From the southern part of the Las Vegas Valley, take Interstate 15 to the Nevada Highway 160 exit (Blue Diamond Road). Head west on Highway 160 for 10 miles, then turn right onto Nevada Highway 159. Drive 6.3 miles past Blue Diamond to the parking lot for First Creek, on the left side of the road.) The trailhead is at the parking area.

Who can resist a hidden waterfall and pool nestled among the trees? This heavenly spot is a favorite for hiker and dog alike. The trek to the falls is across open desert and is an area of choice for the local burros, so keep your eyes out for these wild residents. The falls at First Creek are seasonal, so plan your trip after mountain storms or during spring run-off for the best results.

The well-marked trail begins at the information kiosk and travels across the desert toward the sandstone cliffs. There is a drainage wash to the north (right) that the trail eventually descends into before reaching the falls. Wild burros are often seen and heard in this area. Dogs are usually quite interested in the braying and odors of a nearby burro herd. Bring along a pair of binoculars for a good closeup view of these wild creatures,

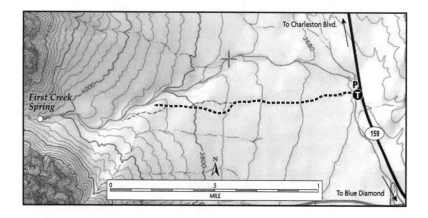

The First Creek area is a favorite with local wild burros.

but remember—do not approach the burros or try to feed them. Wild horses and burros are protected under federal law.

Follow the trail across little hills and valleys as it nears the sandstone bluffs ahead. Just shy of 1 mile into the hike, the trail begins to near the large wash to the north (right). Watch for a small dirt trail that veers off in that direction. Follow this trail down to the wash. A good reference point to look for is a band of brown rock that crosses the wash. Water will drop over this rock and fall 20 feet down into the wash—the waterfall. After a rain, or during times of snowmelt, this waterfall creates a small pool at the base of the falls.

When the weather is fairly mild and the falls are flowing, this area is pure heaven. The shade and relaxing sounds of the water make this portion of the hike the absolute favorite. Plan to spend some time here relaxing with your pooch and soaking up the surroundings. After enjoying the quiet tranquility of the falls, return the way you came or continue up the canyon. This is the end of the designated trail, but people often hike farther up the canyon. If you do this, be aware that the route requires rock scrambling.

26. Ice Box Canyon

Round trip: 2 miles
Elevation range: 4250–5135 feet
Difficulty: Moderate
Hiking time: 1.5 hours
Best canine hiking seasons: Fall through spring
Under foot and paw: Dirt, gravel, rocks, and large boulders
Regulations: Fee area. Dogs must be on a leash 6 feet long or less.
   Waste, including but not limited to dog waste, must be removed
   and disposed of properly.
Map: USGS La Madre Mountain 7.5' quadrangle
Information: Bureau of Land Management, Red Rock Canyon National
   Conservation Area, (702) 515-5350, or *www.redrockcanyon.blm.gov*
Water available: Seasonal waterfall

Getting there: This hike is located off the Red Rock Canyon Scenic Drive in
the Red Rock Canyon National Conservation Area (NCA). From the northern part of the Las Vegas Valley, take Charleston Boulevard west toward the
Spring Mountains. The entrance to the Red Rock Canyon Scenic Drive is on
the north (right) side of the road, approximately 5 miles past the intersection of Charleston Boulevard and State Highway 215 (Las Vegas Beltway).
(Alternate directions: From the southern part of the Las Vegas Valley, take
Interstate 15 to the Nevada Highway 160 exit (Blue Diamond Road). Head
west on Highway 160 for 10 miles, then turn right onto Nevada Highway
159. After 10 miles, turn left into the Red Rock Canyon NCA.) Enter the fee
area and take the Red Rock Canyon Scenic Drive 7.5 miles to the Ice Box
Canyon parking area. The trailhead is at the south side of the parking lot.

For dogs that love to scramble, this hike is pure heaven. The beginning
of the hike is across open desert to warm up the muscles, but when you
enter the canyon it is cool and rocky. "It may sound anthropomorphic

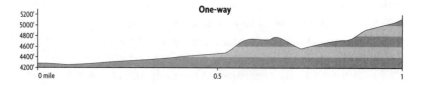

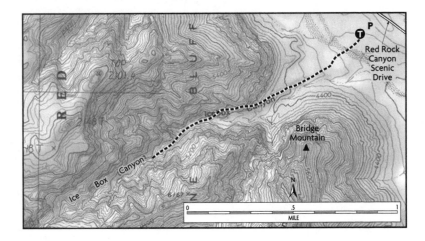

to speak of bored dogs, but animals appear to need environmental stimulations just as humans do." (Katherine A. Houpt and Thomas R. Wolski, *Domestic Animal Behavior*, Iowa State Press, 1982). This hike fits the bill: there are rocks, boulders, bushes, and trees to maneuver around, and seasonal water in the canyon bottom. This trail is an exciting challenge, one that stimulates the dog's mind as well as toning the dog's body.

The hike begins from the obvious trailhead at the edge of the paved parking lot. The beginning of the trail is exposed as you move across the open desert toward the mouth of the canyon. Be prepared for a temperature drop of 10–20°F as you enter the canyon. This canyon was named for its cooler temperatures. The tall, narrow canyon walls shade the area, and cool winds flow down through the canyon from the higher elevations, making a cool respite. In fact, on particularly cool winter days, this area stays a bit too cool and icy to hike.

From the open desert, the trail follows the north (right) side of the canyon along a ridge above the canyon bottom. From here the trail drops into the canyon bottom and the rock-hopping and scrambling begins. (If you miss the turn down into the canyon bottom, it will be obvious when you end up at an impassible rock formation. Turn around and look for the turn down into the canyon.) At this point the trail becomes obscure, but there is no wrong way; just continue up the canyon following the trail if visible.

Although many dogs love rock scrambling and find it a challenge, watch your pet closely to see if it needs some assistance. One common problem on sandstone scrambling routes is the dog's paws and nails. The sandstone acts like sandpaper on the nails, and can wear away skin

Ice Box Canyon was named for its cool temperatures.

on the paws. This trail is particularly hard on dogs' paws and nails, so be sure to bring dog booties and review the information in Part I, under "Health Concerns for Your Dog."

Follow the trail up the canyon. At several places, large boulders limit access and rock scrambling is required. At many of these spots the easiest route around the rockfall isn't obvious; it might take a little investigation to find the best route. After recent rainfall there is a stream, and small pools along the hike.

Along the route it is common to see rock climbers. This is a popular canyon for climbers, due to the cooler temperatures. Many of the small side trails that you see are used by climbers to get back to the canyon walls. It is not uncommon to hear climbers speaking German or Italian high up on the cliffs. Red Rock Canyon NCA is internationally known for its stupendous climbing, and people travel from all over the world to climb these cliffs.

Perhaps the most outstanding part of this hike is the end of the trail. At the back of the canyon the walls close in, forming a natural end to the hike. Here lies an amazing seasonal waterfall. At the base of the falls there is often a pool. Return the way you came, keeping a good eye out for the turn in the trail up out of the wash.

27. Keystone Thrust

Round trip: 2 miles
Elevation range: 4850–5269 feet
Difficulty: Easy
Hiking time: 1–1.5 hours
Best canine hiking seasons: Fall through spring
Under foot and paw: Gravel, dirt, and rock
Regulations: Fee area. Dogs must be on a leash 6 feet long or less. Waste, including but not limited to dog waste, must be removed and disposed of properly.
Map: USGS La Madre Mountain 7.5' quadrangle
Information: Bureau of Land Management, Red Rock Canyon National Conservation Area, (702) 515-5350, or *www.redrockcanyon.blm.gov*
Water available: No

Getting there: This hike is located off the Red Rock Canyon Scenic Drive in the Red Rock Canyon National Conservation Area (NCA). From the

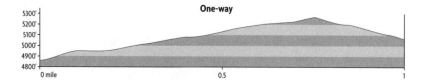

northern part of the Las Vegas Valley, take Charleston Boulevard west toward the Spring Mountains. The entrance to the Red Rock Canyon Scenic Drive is on the north (right) side of the road, approximately 5 miles past the intersection of Charleston Boulevard and State Highway 215 (Las Vegas Beltway). (Alternate directions: From the southern part of the Las Vegas Valley, take Interstate 15 to the Nevada Highway 160 exit (Blue Diamond Road). Head west on Highway 160 for 10 miles, then turn right onto Nevada Highway 159. After 10 miles, turn left into the Red Rock Canyon NCA.) Enter the fee area and take the Red Rock Canyon Scenic Drive 5.8 miles to the White Rock Spring turnoff. Turn right onto a dirt road and drive to the parking lot located at the end of the road.

The Keystone Thrust trail gives the hiker grand views of the area's geology and the thrust fault that gave this hike its name. For your dog, the hike offers an interesting change in scenery. The first portion of the trail weaves through dense desert plants. Later on, the vegetation is sparser as the trail moves across sandstone rock. Please be advised: At the end of the trail there is a significant drop-off, so be careful with your dog in this area. Small pools can form after a rain, so if you plan the trip accordingly your pup may get to splash around.

The trail starts from the north side of the parking area. After a short distance, a trailhead sign marks the Keystone Trail branching off to the right. Throughout the hike, the trail moves from dirt road to trail and back to dirt road again, so watch signs and landmarks carefully.

In this area are many yucca plants. Yuccas are a light green plant with long, sharp, narrow leaves. The native people of the area used these plants extensively for a variety of purposes. The roots of the yucca have a detergent-like quality that made them useful as soaps and shampoos. The leaves were used for fiber to make ropes, cloth, baskets, and shoes. The flowers of the plant were used as food. The tips of the leaves are quite sharp—watch curious pets carefully so they don't get poked.

Along the trail are two roasting pits. Roasting pits are circular areas of fire-cracked and whitened limestone. Native Americans once used the pits to roast foods like agave hearts and desert tortoise. Limestone rocks were gathered, heated by fire, and then left to slow-cook the food. Each time the roasting pits were used the old rocks were scraped back because they would no longer retain heat and new rocks were added to the pits, creating a circular ring. To dogs, the roasting pits probably look like the best digging holes ever! But roasting pits are cultural resources that tell a story of long ago, so make sure to admire them from a distance.

Just over half a mile into the hike, you will get to the top of the hill. The ridge or hill to the right is called Hogback Ridge. Continuing on the main trail, the path turns to the right shortly after the Hogback Ridge turnoff. The gray rock forming the mountains and hills in the surrounding vicinity is limestone, formed 600 to 3100 million years ago when this area lay at the bottom of an ocean. This type of rock is largely composed of fossils of prehistoric marine life. The red and white rock visible farther down the trail is sandstone, formed much later than the limestone. Since the sandstone is a younger rock, it should be closest to the surface. However, geologic movement in the area some 50 to 75 million years ago pushed the gray limestone on top of the red and white

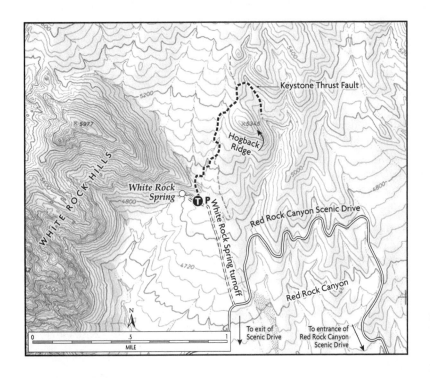

Camy poses at the top of Hogback Ridge.

sandstone, in a movement called a "thrust." The older limestone was thrust over and laid on top of the younger sandstone. This is a significant geological formation that many people come specifically to Red Rock Canyon to see. The Keystone Thrust is a textbook example of a thrust fault (yes—pictures of this hike are actually in textbooks!).

From here, the trail leads downhill to an open sandstone area where the trail vanishes on the hard surface. Turtlehead Peak is clearly visible on the horizon from this view. Continue downslope to a large ravine with a steep drop-off. This is the end of the trail, and a great place to sit and relax with your pooch. After rains, there are small pools in this area that your pup may enjoy splashing around in. Return the way you came.

28. La Madre Spring and Cabin

Round trip: 4.5 miles*
Elevation range: 4590–5731 feet
Difficulty: Moderate
Hiking time: 2.5–3 hours
Best canine hiking seasons: Fall through spring
Under foot and paw: Rocky gravel road, dirt trail, and scattered larger rocks
Regulations: Fee area. Dogs must be on a leash 6 feet long or less. Waste, including but not limited to dog waste, must be removed and disposed of properly.
Map: USGS La Madre Mtn and La Madre Spring 7.5' quadrangles
Information: Bureau of Land Management, Red Rock Canyon National Conservation Area, (702) 515-5350, or *www.redrockcanyon.blm.gov*
Water available: Year-round spring with man-made dam

*3.1 miles if you park at the trailhead instead of at Willow Springs; hiking time 1.5–2 hours

Getting there: This hike is located off the Red Rock Canyon Scenic Drive in the Red Rock Canyon National Conservation Area (NCA). From the northern part of the Las Vegas Valley, take Charleston Boulevard west toward the Spring Mountains. The entrance to the Red Rock Canyon Scenic Drive is on the north (right) side of the road, approximately 5 miles past the intersection of Charleston Boulevard and State Highway 215 (Las Vegas Beltway). (Alternate directions: From the southern part of the Las Vegas Valley, take Interstate 15 to the Nevada Highway 160 exit (Blue Diamond Road). Head west on Highway 160 for 10 miles, then turn right onto Nevada Highway 159. After 10 miles, turn left into the Red Rock Canyon NCA.) Enter the fee area, and take the Red Rock

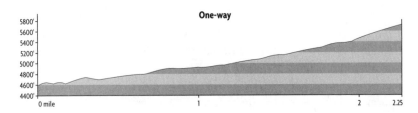

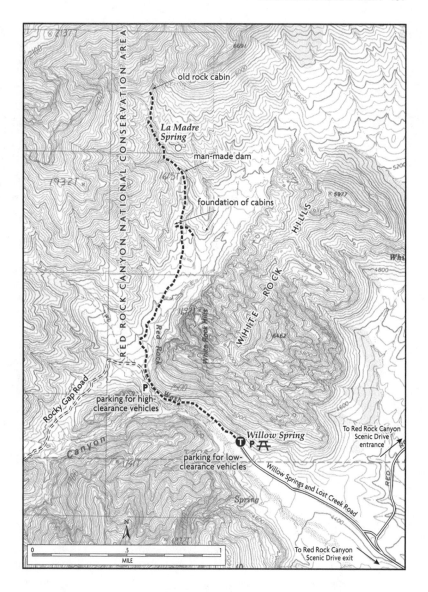

Canyon Scenic Drive 7 miles. Turn right onto Willow Springs and Lost Creek Road. Drive 0.5 mile to the Willow Springs parking lot. If you are traveling in a low-clearance vehicle, park here. Immediately after the Willow Springs area, the paved road ends and becomes a dirt road which is usually passable with a high-clearance vehicle. From Willow Springs, drive 0.7 mile on the dirt road to the trailhead for La Madre

Tracy and Mollie inspect the man-made pond fed by La Madre Spring.

Spring and White Rock. The trailhead is on the right side of the road near several large boulders. On the left side of the dirt road, across from the trailhead, is a parking area.

For dogs that love water, a trail that follows a stream and crosses it multiple times is a true find, particularly in the desert! The La Madre Spring trail offers great scenery, a variety of vegetation habitats, and a slice of history. Also along this hike is a man-made pond that attracts a variety of wildlife. Please be respectful of the bighorn sheep, mule deer, smaller animals, and birds that use this area as one of their primary water sources. While your dog may disagree, the park rangers ask that you not let your dog swim in the pond. Activities like swimming disturb the pond sediments, deteriorating the water quality for the animals that rely on this water source.

From the trailhead, the hike follows an old rocky road on the backside of the White Rock Hills. This hike generally offers solitude, since there are not many people in the area. The views of the backside of the White Rock Hills are very serene. Here the light reflects beautifully off the surrounding hillsides, and sounds of birds chirping are often plentiful, especially first thing in the morning. The vegetation consists of Utah juniper, pinyon pine, Mexican manzanita, and an occasional cactus off the side of the road. After about 1 mile the trail forks, with La Madre Spring to the left and the White Rock–La Madre Spring Loop (Hike 33) to the right. Follow the fork to the left.

About 1.5 miles into the hike are two foundations for old cabins built by a local family that owned the property before it was annexed into Red Rock Canyon NCA. The foundations are not marked, so you have to look around for them. One is on the east side of the trail and one on the west side. The family that built the cabins also owned a tile store in Las Vegas, and remnants of their tile work still remain on the eastern foundation. With permission from the owners, an archery club also used these cabins before they became part of Red Rock Canyon NCA.

Approximately 1.75 miles into the hike, the trail intersects a man-made dam where water from La Madre Spring pools. This point marks a nice change in scenery and vegetation along the hike. Tall reeds and grasses surround the pond. Continue up the trail as it follows along the spring. Dragonflies, birds, wild grapes, columbine flowers, and more tall grasses surround the trail. Even in the middle of summer, this area is surprisingly lush. From here the trail begins to get a little steeper, and in areas the spring creates small waterfalls with moss-covered rocks. Dogs love this area. Crossing a stream, climbing up rocks, and navigating through plants that thickly line the path—what more can a man's best friend ask for?

Eventually the trail emerges out of the lush vegetation. About 2.25 miles into the hike, at about 5731 feet in elevation, the trail reaches an old cabin built primarily out of rocks. The cabin has rock walls 4–5 feet tall, with a roof made of dead branches and tree trunks. Old rusted cans can be found inside the cabin and outside the entryway. This is a great vantage point from which to look back toward the White Rock Hills. Return to your car by retracing your footsteps.

29. Oak Creek Canyon

Round trip: 2–3 miles
Elevation range: 3900–4362 feet
Difficulty: Easy
Hiking time: 1–2 hours
Best canine hiking seasons: Fall through spring
Under foot and paw: Dirt trail and rocky wash
Regulations: Fee area. Dogs must be on a leash 6 feet long or less. Waste, including but not limited to dog waste, must be removed and disposed of properly.
Map: USGS Blue Diamond 7.5' quadrangle
Information: Bureau of Land Management, Red Rock Canyon National Conservation Area, (702) 515-5350, or *www.redrockcanyon.blm.gov*
Water available: No

Getting there: This hike is located off the Red Rock Canyon Scenic Drive in the Red Rock Canyon National Conservation Area (NCA). From the northern part of the Las Vegas Valley, take Charleston Boulevard west toward the Spring Mountains. The entrance to the Red Rock Canyon Scenic Drive is on the north (right) side of the road, approximately 5 miles past the intersection of Charleston Boulevard and State Highway 215 (Las Vegas Beltway). (Alternate directions: From the southern part of the Las Vegas Valley, take Interstate 15 to the Nevada Highway 160 exit (Blue Diamond Road). Head west on Highway 160 for 10 miles, then turn right onto Nevada Highway 159. After 10 miles, turn left into the Red Rock Canyon NCA.) Enter the fee area and take the Red Rock Canyon Scenic Drive 11.3 miles. Turn right onto the dirt road for Oak Creek. Drive 0.7 mile down the dirt road to a parking lot. The trailhead is at the south end of the parking lot. Please note that this hike is also accessible from Nevada Highway 159, but since you would have to unload your dog out of the car right

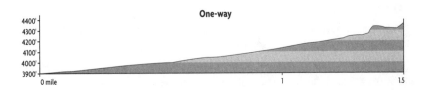

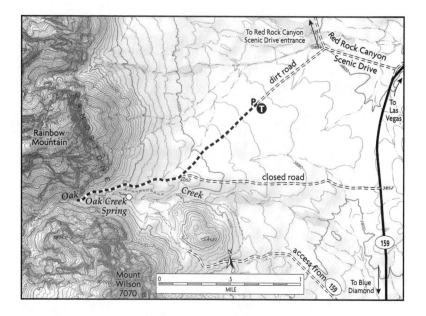

next to a busy road, beginning from the parking lot inside the Red Rock Canyon Scenic Drive is much safer.

The Oak Creek trail is a nice, easy, pleasant hike for you and your dog. It offers scenic views of Rainbow Mountain and Mount Wilson, as well as the Calico Hills on your return trip. The first portion of the trail is well graded, while the second portion is a bit more rugged. This is a great trail to take your dog hiking on, because you can get some easy exercise in the beginning of the hike with a bit of adventure once you are in the canyon.

From the parking lot, the trail begins on the south side near the Oak Creek Trail System sign. The first mile of the hike crosses open desert. Some of the plants to see here include banana yucca, cholla cactus, black bursage, scrub live oak, brittlebush, and cliff rose. The trail through this area is very well graded, and the ground surface is gravel and sand. Almost any dog should be able to complete the hike from the parking lot to the mouth of the canyon. After one mile, the trail begins to enter the canyon. If you are only interested in a short, easy hike, return to the parking lot. If you and your dog would like more of an adventure, continue on into the canyon.

At the mouth of the canyon, the trail runs directly into a wash leading

Camy and Mollie pull Barbara down the hillside.

out of the canyon. The trail continues to the right, staying just above the wash. Continue hiking into the canyon. The farther into the canyon you get, the more rock scrambling is required. Continue exploring the canyon until you feel like returning to your car. To get there, retrace your footsteps.

30. Pine Creek Canyon

Round trip: 2.4 miles
Elevation range: 3953–4177 feet
Difficulty: Easy
Hiking time: 2–3 hours
Best canine hiking seasons: Fall through spring
Under foot and paw: Dirt and gravel
Regulations: Fee area. Dogs must be on a leash 6 feet long or less. Waste, including but not limited to dog waste, must be removed and disposed of properly.
Map: USGS Blue Diamond and La Madre Mountain 7.5' quadrangles
Information: Bureau of Land Management, Red Rock Canyon National Conservation Area, (702) 515-5350, or *www.redrockcanyon.blm.gov*
Water available: Seasonal creek

Getting there: This hike is located off the Red Rock Canyon Scenic Drive in the Red Rock Canyon National Conservation Area (NCA). From the northern part of the Las Vegas Valley, take Charleston Boulevard west toward the Spring Mountains. The entrance to the Red Rock Canyon Scenic Drive is on the north (right) side of the road, approximately 5 miles past the intersection of Charleston Boulevard and State Highway 215 (Las Vegas Beltway). (Alternate directions: From the southern part of the Las Vegas Valley, take Interstate 15 to the Nevada Highway 160 exit (Blue Diamond Road). Head west on Highway 160 for 10 miles, then turn right onto Nevada Highway 159. After 10 miles, turn left into the Red Rock Canyon NCA.) Enter the fee area and take the Red Rock Canyon Scenic Drive 10 miles to the Pine Creek parking area. The trailhead is on the south side of the parking lot.

For you and your pup this is a mellow, enjoyable trail to a historical homestead site, with the opportunity for more extensive hiking beyond

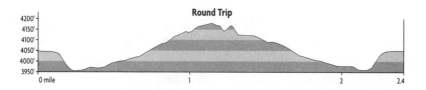

Round Trip

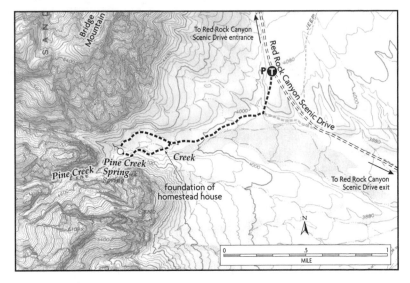

it. Pine Creek Canyon is truly a beautiful hike, winding through the desert to a pine-filled canyon where the foundation of an old homestead house remains. The canyon's trees and a small seasonal creek create a nice shady place for you and your dog to relax while your dog wets its paws. To extend the distance of this hike, there are many options. Try hiking the Fire Ecology Trail, Dale's Trail, or hike into the canyons beyond Pine Creek—all of which spur off the main trail.

The trail begins at a marked trailhead in the parking area. From the parking area, the trail drops down quickly into the desert, then parallels the canyon. After 0.3 mile, the Fire Ecology Trail enters the Pine Creek Trail on the left. This side trail loops around and re-joins the Pine Creek Trail a short distance after the first intersection of the two trails. After 0.4 mile, Dale's Trail enters the Pine Creek Trail. Ice Box Canyon can be accessed via Dale's Trail.

After 0.75 mile the Pine Creek Trail splits into a loop trail. If you look carefully to your left, you will see the foundation of the Wilson homestead. Vandals burned down the home in the early 1960s. Let your dog explore the homestead, and pretend that you have the same view out your front porch.

The Pine Creek area was taken over by the State of Nevada in 1967. The state brought in experts to study the area's biology and geology. They found many unique plant species—some that early settlers planted and some naturally occurring that exist nowhere else in the world. In 1969,

Pine Creek was used to film the movie *Stalking Moon*, with Gregory Peck. Several false-front buildings were erected for the filming of the movie but have long since been disassembled. If you do not see the homestead site as you begin the loop, you will see it on your return path—the trail leads directly by it.

The trail beyond the homestead becomes narrower and trickier to maneuver. This is the part of the trail that your dog will like best. It comes in and out of view with some bushwhacking, rock scrambling, and boulder-hopping required. If you stay to the right, the trail approaches the base of the cliffs and brings you to the entrance of two canyons. If you are interested in a longer hike, you can continue deep into both canyons. If you decide to do this, make sure your dog can handle boulder scrambling. To stay on the regular path, loop around to the left and cross the stream. The trail runs along the southern side of the stream (the stream will be to your left). There are many places along the stream to rest. If your dog is not completely

Pine Creek Canyon offers shade and a cool stream.

transfixed by the water, give it a couple of dog treats, and sit back in the shade for a bit. Eventually, the trail will complete a circle and connect with the original path near the homestead. To return to the parking lot, hike past the homestead and continue on the original trail as you came.

31. Rainbow Springs to Bootleg Spring

Round trip: 7.5 miles*
Elevation range: 4810–5620 feet
Difficulty: Moderate
Hiking time: Year-round
Best canine hiking seasons: Fall and spring
Under foot and paw: Gravel and dirt
Regulations: Dogs must be on a leash 6 feet long or less. Waste, including but not limited to dog waste, must be removed and disposed of properly.
Map: USGS Mountain Springs 7.5' quadrangle
Information: Bureau of Land Management, Red Rock Canyon National Conservation Area, (702) 515-5350, or *www.redrockcanyon.blm.gov*
Water available: Springs and small stream

*1 mile with four-wheel-drive vehicle, with a hiking time of 0.5 hour

Getting there: This hike is located within the Red Rock Canyon National Conservation Area (NCA) but it is not accessed off the Red Rock Canyon Scenic Drive. Take Interstate 15 to the Nevada Highway 160 exit (Blue Diamond Road). Head west on Nevada Highway 160 toward Pahrump. The road will cross over the Spring Mountains in the town of Mountain Springs, and then the road will turn downhill. Three miles past the Mountain Springs Saloon, turn right onto a paved road. This road leads to Lovell Canyon eventually, but you will not be traveling that far. After

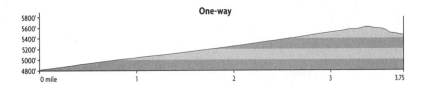

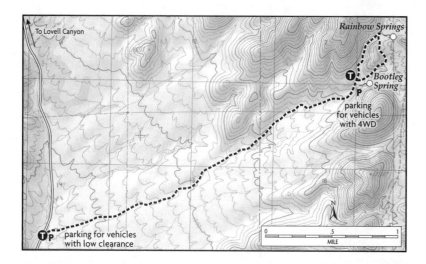

1 mile, a dirt road will enter from the right. Park along the paved road if hiking the whole distance, or continue driving on the dirt road another 2.8 miles if you and your dog are hiking the shorter distance.

This hike is a favorite for its solitude, shade, and water. Rainbow Springs and its neighbor, Bootleg Spring, have good productivity and are running even in the hotter summer months, so water is always available. There is a small pool at Rainbow Springs, not enough for swimming but enough to get some doggie legs wet. Most people have never heard of Rainbow Springs, so chances are you'll be alone on this hike. The moderate elevation makes this area a great in-between-seasons area. When it is a bit too hot in the lower valley but too cold at higher elevations, you and your dog will find that this area is usually perfect in temperature.

Start along the dirt road to the east. After 0.4 mile, the trail will cross a utility line. In this area are many great examples of local plants such as apache plume, Joshua trees, and yuccas. After 1.2 miles, the slight elevation increase changes the ecology of the area, and juniper trees and pinyon pines start becoming evident. After 1.8 miles, the road crosses from Forest Service land onto Bureau of Land Management property.

After 2.8 miles, the road from Bootleg Spring will come in from the right. (This is the place to park for the shorter hike.) From here, the trail loops around from Rainbow Springs to Bootleg Spring and then back to this area. Hike up the main road toward Rainbow Springs. The road quickly narrows, and the water comes into view. Shortly up this trail

Jazmine loves hiking, especially when there's water involved.

there is a small pool where the water from the stream has been dammed up. It is a great place to sit and relax while the dogs get their feet wet. Many different types of wildlife use this area as a water source, so your dog will enjoy all the smells of the surroundings.

Following the stream uphill, the spring source is obscured by a meadow of tall grasses surrounded by a crude wooden fence. From here, there is a small trail leading from the spring to the south (right). The trail goes around a small knoll, and then drops down into the canyon of Bootleg Spring. As you round the knoll, this portion of the Bootleg Canyon is dense in vegetation. Move to the far side of the canyon (south) and you will find a small trail leading down the canyon.

The source of Bootleg Spring is similar to Rainbow Springs in that it is very heavily covered with tall grasses and surrounded by a wooden fence. The trail moves along the south (left) side of the spring and down the canyon. This spring has less water flow than Rainbow Springs, so expect a small stream or trickle down the canyon. This canyon is very narrow and densely shaded. As the trail continues, it widens and eventually reunites with the main road that you came in on. From here, continue back down the road the way you came.

32. Red Rock Escarpment

Round trip: 4.5 miles
Elevation range: 6450–7180 feet
Difficulty: Moderate
Hiking time: 3.5–4.5 hours
Best canine hiking seasons: Fall through spring
Under foot and paw: Dirt, sandstone
Regulations: Fee area. Dogs must be on a leash 6 feet long or less. Waste, including but not limited to dog waste, must be removed and disposed of properly.
Map: USGS La Madre Spring 7.5' quadrangle
Information: Bureau of Land Management, Red Rock Canyon National Conservation Area, (702) 515-5350, or *www.redrockcanyon.blm.gov*
Water available: No

Getting there: This hike is located off the Red Rock Canyon Scenic Drive in the Red Rock Canyon National Conservation Area (NCA). From the northern part of the Las Vegas Valley, take Charleston Boulevard west toward the Spring Mountains. The entrance to the Red Rock Canyon Scenic Drive is on the north (right) side of the road, approximately 5 miles past the intersection of Charleston Boulevard and State Highway 215 (Las Vegas Beltway). (Alternate directions: From the southern part of the Las Vegas Valley, take Interstate 15 to the Nevada Highway 160 exit (Blue Diamond Road). Head west on Highway 160 for 10 miles, then turn right onto Nevada Highway 159. After 10 miles, turn left into the Red Rock Canyon NCA.) Enter the fee area and take the Red Rock Canyon Scenic Drive 7 miles. Turn right onto Willow Springs and Lost Creek Road. Immediately after the Willow Springs area, the paved road ends and becomes a dirt road called Rocky Gap Road. This dirt road is usually passable with a vehicle that has a short wheelbase

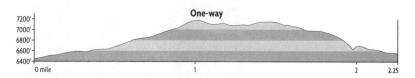

and high clearance; however, four-wheel drive is recommended. Since the road conditions are constantly changing, particularly after a rainstorm, it is best to ask the park rangers at the visitor center for updated road conditions. Another thing to consider is whether your dog gets carsick. This is a bumpy, windy road that may upset a sensitive dog's stomach. From the end of the pavement, it is 4.8 miles to the trailhead and summit of the road. On the left side of the road are a parking area and trailhead sign. Please note that the road does continue downhill, and eventually connects with Nevada Highway 160 to get back to Las Vegas, but the downhill portion of the Rocky Gap Road is not maintained and conditions are generally much rougher than from Willow Springs to the summit.

This is an excellent hike to the top of the escarpment above Pine Creek. The trail leads through Utah juniper, Mexican manzanita, and agave before it drops down into a beautiful sandstone rock area that is the top of the escarpment.

While this really is a great hike, there are several important things to be aware of. First, this trail extends to Bridge Mountain, an area with a sandstone bridge formation. The hike described here stops at the escarpment. The trek onward to Bridge Mountain from the escarpment requires serious rock scrambling and balance; it has extreme drop-offs that cannot be avoided. So while it is an exhilarating trek for two-legged people, it is not at all recommended for those hiking with four-legged friends. Second, since this hike goes to the top of the escarpment, although the trail does not teeter along the edge, there are sheer drop-offs. So keeping your dog under strict control is essential. With that said, this really is a nice, enjoyable hike and there are rarely many people in this area of Red Rock Canyon NCA.

From the trailhead, begin to hike uphill. The trail leads through a pinyon-juniper plant community, with quite a few Utah agave plants. Along the trail, the tall agave stalks will particularly catch your eye. The Utah agave plant has a rosette of thick bluish leaves with marginal teeth or spines growing from a tight base. In April or May, the plant sends up a rapidly growing stalk with clusters of thin yellow flowers. Within 30 days, the stalk can grow 15 feet tall! After the stalk has shot up, the plant dies. Native Americans once collected this plant and roasted it in a communal pit for days. (Many of the pits can be seen at lower elevations in Red Rock.) Once cooked, the hearts of the agave plant are dark and sweet, and taste like molasses.

Opposite: Great rock scrambling is just around the corner.

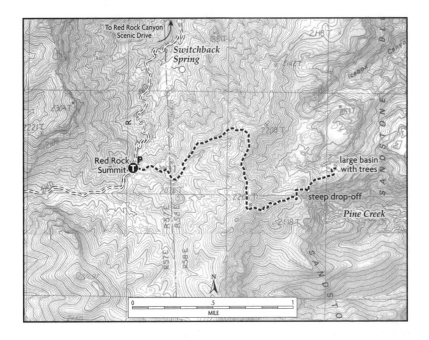

After about 1 mile, the trail reaches a T intersection where views of the Las Vegas Valley are first visible. Down below are sandstone rocks with colors varying among red, burgundy, pink, yellow, and white. In the distance, the James Hardie gypsum mining operation is plainly visible. The trail heading north (left) from the intersection leads to North Peak. The trail to the south (right) is marked as the Bridge Mountain Trail. It loops around the hillside to the south and ends up on the sandstone down below. Follow the trail to the right toward Bridge Mountain and the escarpment.

After passing more juniper and pine trees, the trail loops around and reaches the southern end of the sandstone outcrop. At this point, start to be more aware of drop-offs and make sure your dog does not go exploring too close to the edge. The trail continues downhill, switchbacking toward the white sandstone. The trail soon changes from well-compacted dirt to sandstone. As the trail switchbacks across the sandstone, it can be tricky to follow. Try to follow the areas of compacted rock. There are usually a few rock cairns along the way.

About 2 miles into the hike, the trail brings you to the escarpment. Have your hiking buddy hold your dog by the leash away from the edge, and go look down at Pine Creek, about 1500 feet below. Here you have a completely new perspective of the canyons. The view is quite spectacular.

For the remainder of the hike, continue exploring with your dog in a northeastern direction. For the most part, there are no more cliffs for the remainder of the hike. The trail continues across a series of slick sandstone benches, again marked by rock cairns. This is a fun area for dogs to explore since it is not a strict path that they have to stick to. Depending on the season and recent weather events, there are often several basins that collect water here. The largest basin is shown on the topographic map as the end of the hike. Once you are on the sandstone benches, look for a large, dead, black pine tree sticking up, roughly to your left. It has been hit by lightning and has few branches. It stands near the basin, so make your way toward the tree and loop around to the right of it to get down into the basin. Your dog will have fun running and climbing up the sandstone benches. When there is water pooled up, the basin is like a mini-oasis. This is a popular spot for wild animals and birds to get a drink.

The basin marks the end of the hike. The mountain to the northeast from the basin is Bridge Mountain. If you look carefully, you can see the sandstone bridge. To get back to your car and the Rocky Gap Road, retrace your footsteps.

33. White Rock–La Madre Spring Loop

Round trip: 5.9 miles
Elevation range: 4383–5519 feet
Difficulty: Moderate
Hiking time: 3 hours
Best canine hiking seasons: Fall through spring
Under foot and paw: Dirt and gravel, short portion paved
Regulations: Dogs must be on a leash 6 feet long or less. Waste, including but not limited to dog waste, must be removed and disposed of properly.
Map: USGS La Madre Mtn and La Madre Spring 7.5' quadrangles
Information: Bureau of Land Management, Red Rock Canyon National Conservation Area, (702) 515-5350, or *www.redrockcanyon.blm.gov*
Water available: Small man-made catchment off the main trail

Getting there: This hike is located off the Red Rock Canyon Scenic Drive in the Red Rock Canyon National Conservation Area (NCA). From the

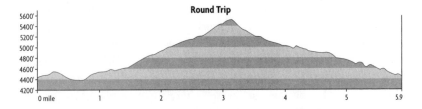

northern part of the Las Vegas Valley, take Charleston Boulevard west toward the Spring Mountains. The entrance to the Red Rock Canyon Scenic Drive is on the north (right) side of the road, approximately 5 miles past the intersection of Charleston Boulevard and State Highway 215 (Las Vegas Beltway). (Alternate directions: From the southern part of the Las Vegas Valley, take Interstate 15 to the Nevada Highway 160 exit (Blue Diamond Road). Head west on Highway 160 for 10 miles, then turn right onto Nevada Highway 159. After 10 miles, turn left into the Red Rock Canyon NCA.) Enter the fee area and take the Red Rock Canyon Scenic Drive 7 miles. Turn right onto Willow Springs and Lost Creek Road. Park in the Lost Creek parking lot, which is the first parking lot on the left.

Gotta love those loop hikes! It really makes each portion of a trail new and exciting when you don't have to return along the same trail. This diverse hike is a favorite for our canine companions. It loops around White Rock Hills and passes through a traditional desert environment around to juniper and pine trees. The curves and hills keep this trail fun and varied.

From the parking lot, look across the road to the hillside. The trail going up the hill to the right is the White Rock–La Madre Spring Loop trail. Follow this trail up the hill over the ridge. The trail moves down across hills and washes below the White Rock Hills on the west (left) side, then heads north and steadily uphill toward the White Rock Spring parking area. As you near the parking area, a trail comes in from the west (left). This short side trail takes you to White Rock Spring, a small water source captured in a man-made catchment. Let your dog get a drink out of the catchment. Don't be surprised if you see goldfish in there. Some people have had the not-so-bright idea of putting goldfish in the catchment. While this may be a cute idea, doing so jeopardizes the water quality for wild animals that use the spring as a water source. There is shade in this area, so if it is time for a snack or lunch break, this is a good spot for it.

Continue back up the hill toward the parking area. There are restrooms at the parking lot if needed. From the circular parking area at White Rock, continue hiking on the trail to the north. Shortly after leaving the White Rock parking area, the trail to Keystone Thrust (Hike 27) branches off to the right. Continue on the main trail heading west (left) as you and your dog continue the journey of looping around the White Rock Hills. As the trail winds around the backside of the White Rock Hills, it moves up ridges and down into drainages. The constant small elevation changes keep this hike moderately strenuous.

The terrain eventually changes from open desert to pines and juniper. Even the pooches welcome this change, for there is shade available and the zone change creates new smells to take in. As you move around the northernmost point of the loop and start heading south on the backside of the White Rock Hills, you are given some spectacular views of the hillside and canyon below. This is a view that few people, let alone dogs, experience. The solitude is enjoyable here, and there are lots of little birdies for your dog to listen to.

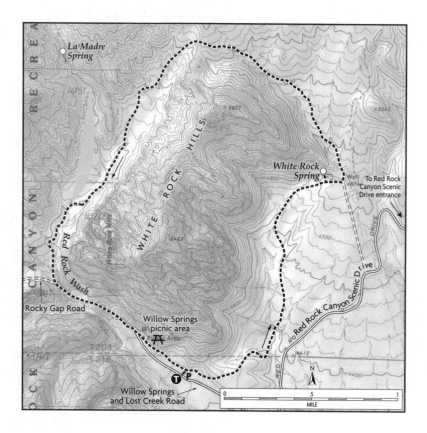

About half way around the backside of the White Rock Hills, the trail intersects the old dirt road that leads to the La Madre Spring and Cabin (Hike 28). The La Madre Spring area is to the north (right), but the White Rock–La Madre Spring Loop hike continues downhill to the south (left). Continue leading your dog south. At the southern end of the White Rock Hills, the trail will intersect the Rocky Gap Road, another dirt road. Turn (west) left onto the Rocky Gap Road and walk toward the Lost Creek–Willow Springs area. Once you reach the Willow Springs picnic area, the road is paved. The Willow Springs picnic area is a popular destination in Red Rock Canyon NCA. With large trees, shaded picnic tables, grills, trash receptacles, and restrooms, it is an attractive lunch stop for many weekend visitors driving the Red Rock Canyon Scenic Drive. During the week, schoolchildren on field trips snack here as well. Continue walking along the paved road to the Lost Creek parking lot and your car.

Desert plants are found on the east side of the loop.

SPRING MOUNTAINS NATIONAL RECREATION AREA (MOUNT CHARLESTON)

All of us who love spending time outdoors hold a special fondness for the Spring Mountains National Recreation Area (NRA). Known to locals as Mount Charleston, the Spring Mountains NRA offers a change in temperature and surroundings at all times of the year. During the summer, when it is blazing hot in town, it may be 70° or 80°F at Mount Charleston. During the winter when you are looking for something fun to do, there is snow at Mount Charleston—so you can go skiing, sledding, and snowshoeing in the desert!

The U.S. Forest Service manages the Spring Mountains NRA, which encompasses 316,000 acres, making it the third largest National Recreational Area in the National Forest system. The Spring Mountains NRA is part of the larger Toiyabe National Forest. Elevations in the area range from 4500 feet in the high desert to 11,918 feet at the top of Mount Charleston Peak, so there is a great amount of biodiversity. As you drive up Kyle Canyon to some of the hikes listed in this book, you pass through five of the six North American life zones. You can only do this in a handful of places across the continent! There are also 80 named springs or seeps

Kristi and Tracy take Sida and Mollie for a summer hike at Mount Charleston.

that help support a variety of wildlife, including quail, turkey, deer, elk, wild horses, and burros. Like other natural places around the valley, this area is home to many species that are considered threatened, endangered or sensitive. In fact, there are 57 species in the Spring Mountains NRA that are endemic—they live nowhere else in the world.

As you explore the mountain, be aware that an unusual feature of this area is that residential property is in close proximity to the public lands. Remember to respect the private landholder, and venture only on public lands.

There are many good hiking trails in the Spring Mountains NRA, some of which are maintained by the U.S. Forest Service, and many of which are not. At the request of the U.S. Forest Service, we are only including maintained trails in this book. Conditions on these trails are consistently maintained, keeping them safe for you and your dog. Also, since there are so many sensitive plants in the Spring Mountains NRA, hiking on these trails keeps you and your dog from inadvertently disturbing any of these plants. The U.S. Forest Service is studying many of the user-created trails that have become quite popular. In the future, they plan on converting some of these trails into maintained trails, once they have determined that such an action is appropriate. For the time being, please try and stick to the maintained trails, including all the ones described in this book.

34. Bonanza Trail (Spring Mountains Divide Trail)

Round trip: 32 miles*
Elevation range: 7534–10,284 feet
Difficulty: Difficult
Hiking time: Overnight backpacking trip
Best canine hiking seasons: Spring through fall
Under foot and paw: Dirt and gravel
Regulations: Dogs must be on a leash 6 feet long or less. Waste must be removed and disposed of properly.
Map: USGS Charleston Peak, Wheeler Well, Willow Peak, and Cold Creek 7.5' quadrangles
Information: United States Forest Service, Spring Mountains National Recreation Area, (702) 515-5400 and (in emergencies) (702) 872-5306, or *www.fs.fed.us/r4/htnf/districts/smnra/index.shtml*
Water available: Seasonally at spring

*16 miles one-way, using two cars, one parked at each end of the trail; hiking time 10 hours

Getting there: Take US Highway 95 north out of Las Vegas. About 20 miles past the Ann Road exit, turn west onto Nevada Highway 156 toward Mount Charleston's Lee Canyon area. Continue on Highway 156 for approximately 17.25 miles until you reach the Lee Canyon ski area parking lot. Park at the top portion of the parking area near the turnaround.

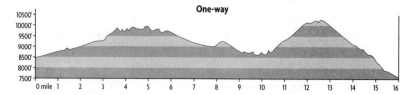

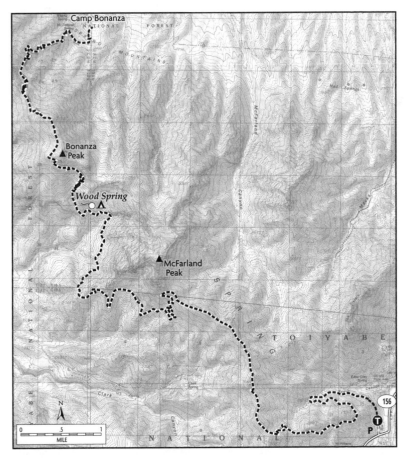

There are not many established long trails around Las Vegas, and for this reason this hike is an exceptional treat and a great challenge for you and your dog. Also known as the Spring Mountains Divide Trail, the Bonanza Trail takes you across the ridgelines from Lee Canyon to Cold Creek. The hike is not easy—it is long, with a lot of elevation gains and losses—but it is a fun challenge with amazing views from the ridge down into the valleys to the east and west. Be certain that your dog is ready for this level of physical challenge. It is a long way to carry a tired dog if you are wrong! This trail can be done round trip as an overnight hike, with a great backpacking site including a small spring and camp area. Or it can be a long one-way hike using two cars, one parked at each end of the trail. If you do this, the hike is reduced to 16 miles.

When it comes to longer hikes at Mount Charleston, most think of the Mount Charleston loop trail. Although lesser-known, the dramatic Bonanza Trail is definitely worthwhile.

The hike begins along the Bristlecone Trail (Hike 35) at an elevation of 8418 feet. The majority of this hike is at 8000 feet or above, so make sure you and your pet are ready for the elevation. When you are not used to high elevation it puts increased pressure on your body. The air is thinner, so you must breathe more rapidly to acquire enough oxygen for your system. By keeping a slow and steady pace, you can usually keep the effects of the altitude to a minimum. Signs of altitude sickness include a general sense of tiredness, loss of appetite, and headache. More severely, nausea and dizziness can occur. Symptoms are remedied by retreating to lower elevations.

The beginning portion of the trail is a closed road lined on either side with pines and aspens. In the fall, this area is full of color. Continue along the Bristlecone Trail for 2.9 miles until intersecting the Bonanza Trail to the northwest. The intersection is signed.

From here the trail narrows and switchbacks for 3 miles as it rises in elevation, then rides across the ridgeline until nearing the McFarland Peak area. Other hikers are scarce on the portion of the trail from here until Cold Creek, which will give you and your pooch plenty of solitude. As you near McFarland Peak, the trail turns south, west, and later north as it moves

Overnight travelers can stay at the campsite near Wood Spring.

its way around the mountain. The trail has a fair share of twists and turns and elevation ups and downs, keeping the hike challenging but stimulating. Your pooch will find this hike full of new sights and smells; don't be surprised if your dog is pulling at the end of the leash the whole way.

Between McFarland Peak and Bonanza Peak is a very small spring called Wood Spring. The output is minimal, but could be essential if you have underestimated your water needs. The water does need to be purified before use. In this spot is also a camp area with a fire pit for overnight travelers. The area is flat and somewhat protected.

From this area, the trail continues on toward Bonanza Peak. As with McFarland, the trail skirts around the peak to the west and continues its trek to the north. As you near Cold Creek, the trail switchbacks extensively to reduce elevation. This area at Cold Creek often has wild horses grazing near the parking area, so keep a lookout for these majestic animals. This is the end of the one-way hike; if you are hiking round trip, return the way you came.

35. Bristlecone Loop

Round trip: 6-mile loop*
Elevation range: 8415–9320 feet
Difficulty: Moderate
Hiking time: 3–4 hours
Best canine hiking seasons: Spring through fall
Under foot and paw: Dirt trail, old dirt road
Regulations: Dogs must be on a leash 6 feet long or less. Waste must be removed and disposed of properly.
Map: USGS Charleston Peak 7.5' quadrangle
Information: United States Forest Service, Spring Mountains National Recreation Area, (702) 515-5400 and (in emergencies) (702) 872-5306, or *www.fs.fed.us/r4/htnf/districts/smnra/index.shtml*
Water available: No

*5 miles if using two cars, one parked at the Lee Canyon ski area and one parked off Canyon Road.

Getting there: Take US Highway 95 north out of Las Vegas. About 20 miles past the Ann Road exit, turn west onto Nevada Highway 156 toward

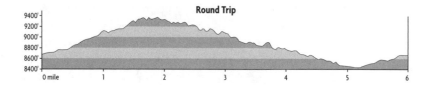

Mount Charleston's Lee Canyon area. Continue on Highway 156 for approximately 17.25 miles until you reach the Lee Canyon ski area parking lot. Park at the top portion of the parking area near the turnaround. The trailhead is located at the west side of the parking lot. To hike the shorter distance (5 miles), from the intersection of US Highway 95 and Nevada Highway 156, drive up the mountain 16.5 miles on Nevada Highway 156. Turn north (right) on Canyon Road, which is about 140 feet north of the McWilliams Campground. Ample parking is available. Drive the second car to the Lee Canyon ski area to start the hike.

This hike is a favorite for hiker and dog alike. The plant and wildlife diversity, as well as the views along the trail, keep the hike interesting. Your dog will enjoy moving from deep forests to a ridgeline, and finally to an old road that has long since been closed. In the fall, the aspen leaves turn a spectacular golden yellow. As the trail's name implies, here you can see bristlecone pines, known for being one of the longest-living organisms in the world. Although there is no water available along the trail, the first portion of the hike is heavily shaded, and the cooler temperatures at these elevations keep the pooches cool and content.

The hike begins at the upper Lee Canyon ski area parking lot. The trail kiosk is located at the paved turnaround/helicopter landing site at the top of the parking lot. From the kiosk, the trail immediately heads uphill along a small ridge. Off to the left are views of the Lee Canyon ski area. The ski runs are clearly visible, and golden aspen stands are easy to spot in the fall.

As the trail continues through the forest, it moves through the occasional aspen stand, giving close-up views of the beautiful white-barked, golden-leaved trees. Throughout this first portion of the hike, the trail is narrow and well shaded. The trail meanders upward slowly, increasing in elevation. At this point, wondering where you are going, your dog should be awfully excited.

The next section of the hike moves along a ridgeline, giving magnificent views of Lee Canyon below. Take a break when you get here, and let your dog sniff the fresh air coming up from the canyon below. Keep your eyes open for a stand of bristlecone pines in this area. The bristlecone pine is a short tree, in comparison to other pine trees, and it has a twisted trunk. These trees are commonly found on high, exposed slopes. The arrangement of needles around the branches creates the illusion that the branch is a bristly animal's tail. These trees can live to be several thousand years old. The needles are pointy, so make sure your dog doesn't get poked if you are standing close to a tree examining it!

As the hike moves around the canyon to loop back, the trail joins an old dirt road that has long been closed. In this area, the trail is more exposed with less shade available but it has very even terrain. If the weather is warm, make sure you and your dog are drinking plenty of water. It may be a good time to reapply sunscreen as well. There are tremendous views down into the bowl of Lee Canyon from here.

As the trail descends slowly down the incline, it makes its way back

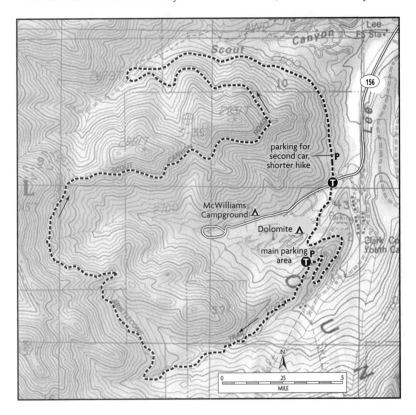

Everybody loves a loop hike!

into the trees. The shade will be welcome to you and your dog. In this area, the trail remains wide with more aspen stands. When the trail opens up to a dirt parking area, Nevada Highway 156 and Canyon Road are near. If you parked a second car off Canyon Road, your hike terminates here. If you parked at the Lee Canyon ski resort, follow Nevada Highway 156 uphill to the parking lot.

36. Cathedral Rock

Round trip: 2.8 miles
Elevation range: 7630–8550 feet
Difficulty: Moderately strenuous
Hiking time: 2–3 hours
Best canine hiking seasons: Spring through fall
Under foot and paw: Gravel with small rocks, sometimes slightly
   slick
Regulations: Dogs must be on a leash 6 feet long or less. Waste must
   be removed and disposed of properly.
Map: USGS Charleston Peak 7.5' quadrangle
Information: United States Forest Service, Spring Mountains
   National Recreation Area, (702) 515-5400 and (in emergencies)
   (702) 872-5306, or *www.fs.fed.us/r4/htnf/districts/smnra/index.shtml*
Water available: Seasonal waterfall

Getting there: Take US Highway 95 north out of Las Vegas. 5.4 miles past the Ann Road exit, turn west onto Nevada Highway 157 toward Mount Charleston's Kyle Canyon area. Follow Nevada Highway 157 up to Kyle Canyon. Roughly 3 miles past the Kyle Canyon Visitor Center, Nevada Highway 157 will make an extreme left turn, and an adjoining road will continue straight ahead into a residential area. Follow Nevada Highway 157 as it curves to the left. After about 0.3 mile, there will be a parking area on your right.

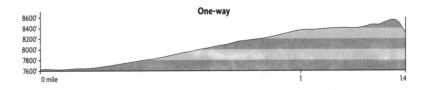

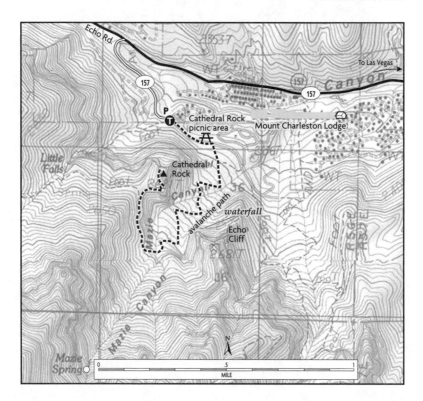

The Cathedral Rock Trail is a moderately strenuous hike to the top of a 1000-foot limestone rock face, so this hike is only recommended for fit dogs that can handle a substantial elevation gain in a short distance. This trail has much to offer, including colorful wildflowers during the summer months and one of the best displays of fall color anywhere around Las Vegas. In the fall, yellow aspen trees surrounding the trail are a good reminder that there actually are seasons in Las Vegas. For your dog, this trail has the added bonus of a seasonal waterfall about halfway up the trail. When you reach the summit, pay close attention to your dog—there is a sheer drop-off at the edge of the summit. This hike is not recommended when there is snow on the trail or at higher elevations. The trail leads through an area historically known for avalanches.

There are two trailheads for this hike. The first one is from the parking lot just before the Mount Charleston Lodge and Cathedral Rock Picnic Area. The hike description given below begins from here. The second trailhead is from inside the Cathedral Rock Picnic Area. Be aware there is a $6.00 fee for the use of the picnic area. If you choose to begin the hike

from inside the picnic area, the trailhead is located at the first parking lot inside the fee area. Check with the rangers to determine the time the picnic area closes so your vehicle does not get locked in.

From the parking lot, head up the stairs and follow the well-marked trail to the left. The trail leads through ponderosa pines and white fir, but it soon enters a stand of aspen trees. During the summer, this portion of the trail is lined with wildflowers; during the fall, the aspen leaves turn a golden yellow. This portion of the trail is in a major avalanche path where many snow slides have occurred during the winter months. The snow slides prevent the pine trees and white fir from growing here, leaving the area open to the quicker-growing aspen trees and seasonal flowers. At the beginning of the hike, the trail comes to a junction with a trail coming in from the campground. At the junction continue heading uphill, to the right.

About 0.6 mile in on the trail, there is an old road that leads to a waterfall just off the left side of the trail. Early in the spring there are three falls flowing down, but by late summer the water has usually dried up. If water is available, this is a good spot for your dog to cool down and get a drink. Make sure that you are carrying enough water for your pooch in case the waterfall has already dried out for the season.

Along the way to the top of Cathedral Rock, stop and contemplate the history of the rock face in front of you. In 1959, a man by the name of "Doc" Bayley, owner and developer of the Hacienda Hotel Corporation, owned about 1400 acres of private property within Kyle Canyon, including the Mount Charleston Resort Lodge and all the private land on both sides of the highway from the Kyle Canyon Visitor Center to the base of Cathedral Rock. Bayley had grand plans for the area, including a Mount Rushmore-style carving-out of Cathedral Rock. Initially, the plan was to carve out the busts of four Navy chaplains. During World War II, these four men gave their life preservers to four soldiers so that they could survive after their U-boat was torpedoed off of Newfoundland. About 600 of the 900 troops on board drowned, including the four chaplains. Witnesses reported seeing the four chaplains standing with their arms linked together as the ship went down. Before Bayley could execute his plans, he died of a heart attack, leaving his wife Judy in charge of his project. Judy Bayley eventually decided that a carving of a more current hero would be more suitable, so she started plans to hire a sculptor to carve

Opposite: Doug and Mollie hike through golden fall colors.

out a bust of John F. Kennedy. Before any work began, Judy Bayley sold the property and the new owners decided not to pursue the Mount Rushmore idea. As you ascend Cathedral Rock, can you imagine the faces carved in the cliff?

As the trail reaches the backside of Cathedral Rock, keep to the right. The trail climbs several short and steep switchbacks before it reaches the summit. The view down Kyle Canyon is very impressive. From the summit you can look straight down on the Mount Charleston Lodge and all the communities in Kyle Canyon. While at the summit, remember to keep your dog a safe distance away from the edge. When you are done enjoying the view and perhaps having a picnic, return to your car by retracing your path.

37. Cave Spring via Trail Canyon

Round trip: 5 miles
Elevation range: 7813–9834 feet
Difficulty: Moderate
Hiking time: 3 hours
Best canine hiking seasons: Spring through fall
Under foot and paw: Gravel and dirt
Regulations: Dogs must be on a leash 6 feet long or less. Waste must be removed and disposed of properly.
Map: USGS Charleston Peak 7.5' quadrangle
Information: United States Forest Service, Spring Mountains National Recreation Area, (702) 515-5400 and (in emergencies) (702) 872-5306, or *www.fs.fed.us/r4/htnf/districts/smnra/index.shtml*
Water available: Trough of water

Getting there: Take US Highway 95 north for 5.4 miles past Ann Road to the Route 157 turn-off. Turn left (west) onto Route 157 and head

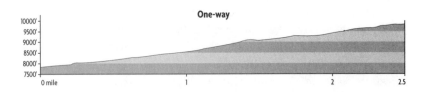

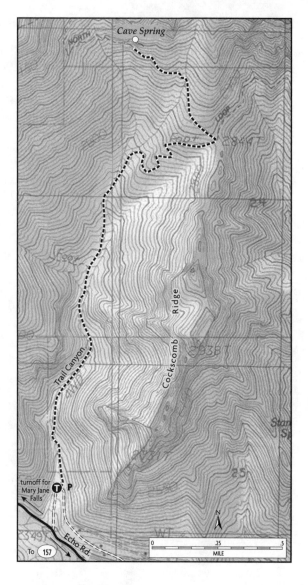

up the hill. Approximately 2.2 miles after the Kyle Canyon Ranger Station, the road will make an extreme left. Instead of following it to the left, continue straight onto Echo Road. Continue on Echo Road until it makes an extreme right turn. Park your vehicle in the unpaved parking area at the bend in the road. The trailhead sign for Trail Canyon will be obvious—it is right next to the parking area.

With a decent elevation change and some fantastic views, the hike to Cave Spring is a challenge, but worth the work. Your dog will be excited when you get to the end of the trail and discover a water trough fed by the Cave Spring. The trail is well defined and easy to follow, with abundant shade available. The trail is mainly dirt with small gravel-sized rocks, so it should be rather easy on your dog's paws.

The trail begins at the kiosk next to the parking area. This trail climbs 2000 feet in 2.5 miles so expect a good workout. Initially the trail is gravel, but it changes to dirt farther along the route. The trail moves in and out of aspen groves and pine areas, so there is plenty of shade to rest in if you or your dog is out of breath from the climb. As you increase in elevation, take a few moments to turn around and take in the view. As you look back toward Kyle Canyon, you see beautiful rock formations and valley vistas.

Just shy of 2 miles into the hike, the trail forks to the left and right. The trail to the left takes you to Cave Spring, the right toward Mummy Springs (Hike 41). Turn left toward Cave Spring. The trail moves through a burnt area where a fire occurred over fifty years ago. The burnt trees remain, but there is fresh young growth around them. Aspen trees are fast-growing and commonly occur soon after a major disturbance like a fire or landslide, so you will see many of them surrounding the burnt landscape. During fire succession, faster-growing trees and shrubs become established first, and are later replaced by slower-growing species.

If your dog likes water, start pepping it up because the trail inclines slowly toward the spring. The spring site is easy to spot; there is a trough made out of a large log that catches water piped from the spring. Splash water onto your dog's belly to cool it down and get it excited. Trees keep the area shaded and create a bit of shelter. This is a great dog-biscuit dining area and rest stop. The dogs will appreciate the water and the shade. The water in the trough needs to be purified for drinking.

This is the end of the Cave Spring hike. From here, return to your vehicle. It is all downhill from here! The trail that leads beyond Cave Spring is the trail to Mount Charleston Peak. Maybe try the peak on another day. . . .

Opposite: A wooden trough carved from a tree trunk collects water.

38. Fletcher Canyon

Round trip: 3.2 miles
Elevation range: 6931–7935 feet
Difficulty: Moderate
Hiking time: 2–3 hours
Best canine hiking seasons: Spring through fall
Under foot and paw: Dirt and some gravel
Regulations: Dogs must be on a leash 6 feet long or less. Waste must
   be removed and disposed of properly.
Map: USGS Angel Peak 7.5' quadrangle
Information: United States Forest Service, Spring Mountains
   National Recreation Area, (702) 515-5400 and (in emergencies)
   (702) 872-5306, or *www.fs.fed.us/r4/htnf/districts/smnra/index.shtml*
Water available: Seasonal creek

Getting there: Take US Highway 95 north out of Las Vegas. 5.4 miles past
the Ann Road exit, turn west onto Nevada Highway 157 toward Mount
Charleston. Follow Nevada Highway 157 up to Kyle Canyon. A half-mile
past the turn-off to Nevada Highway 158 is the Fletcher Canyon trailhead.
The trailhead is hard to see and the parking is on the south (left) side of
the road, so a great alternative is to drive another 0.1 mile to the visitor
center and turn around. The parking is on the south (right if heading
downhill) side of the road, in two pullouts near the trailhead.

This is truly one of the best hikes in this area, and one that can be done
over and over. Besides being a nice casual hike through the woods, it has
a spring and a narrow canyon area to explore. There are a host of interesting plants, insects, birds, and animals along this hike. The diversity of
wildlife in the canyon makes this a fun and interesting walk for people
and dogs of all ages. It is not uncommon to see something new every
time you take this trek. The Mount Charleston area commonly gets more

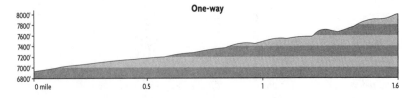

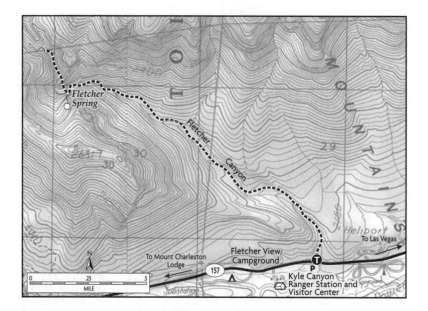

storms than the Las Vegas Valley. Keep weather in mind when hiking up into this narrow canyon environment. Strong water flows etched this canyon out of the rock, and flash floods are still a danger, so stay away if rain is in the forecast.

The trail begins on the north side of the road next to a U.S. Forest Service information board. The parking pullouts are right next to the road, so watch dogs carefully as they exit the vehicle and cross the road to the trailhead. This trail is popular with visitors to the Mount Charleston area. Many start the trail, but few venture back to the rockfall areas in the Fletcher narrows.

The trail moves immediately up-canyon from the trailhead. For this portion of the hike to the stream crossing, the trail is fairly wide and well maintained. The hike begins on the left of a wash and then crosses the wash. The trail continues on the right side of the wash for some distance. Depending on water availability, the wash commonly has a small stream running through it so the pups can get their feet wet and splash around a bit.

Pine trees and scrub oak are abundant, so the trail is shaded throughout much of the hike. In places along the trail you can see rusty pipe from long ago when the spring was piped downhill for the Kyle Sawmill. Wood from the sawmill was hauled down into Las Vegas to build some of the first buildings in the valley.

Columbine at Fletcher Canyon (Photo by Ryan Hewitt)

The vegetation changes in this canyon will definitely catch your attention. Throughout the first portion of the hike there are cacti among the pines looking somewhat out of place at this elevation. Around the spring there are columbine, maidenhair fern, and wild rose growing in abundance. Your dog will enjoy sniffing around the different plants, trying to pick up the scent of chipmunks or other animals that may have passed by. This canyon is also known for having many different species of butterflies. It is also popular with hummingbirds, so keep your eye out for their small, cupped nests. If you see one, keep your distance. The mother hummingbird will be very territorial, circling her nest and swooping past you and your dog as if saying, "Get back and leave my babies alone!"

Farther up the canyon, the trail crosses the stream. This is a great area for a picnic—there is abundant shade, and often wildflowers along the stream. The trail up to this point is considered easy. From here, the remainder of the hike is moderate due to rock-scrambling terrain.

From the stream heading north, the trail narrows and becomes harder to find against the natural terrain. The hike moves up into a true canyon environment with high canyon walls, which are quite breathtaking. There are several places where rock scrambling is necessary, so let your dog jump from rock to rock. At the end of the trail there is a large rock formation with a rockslide worn into the stone over years of water flow through the area. The first portion by the rockslide can be climbed but just past it is a larger rock formation that blocks the canyon, marking the end of the hike. Some dogs may not be able to get past the rockslide. Since there is not much to see beyond it, there is no sense in pushing them too hard. After some fun climbing the rocks or resting by the stream, return the way you came.

39. Griffith Peak via Harris Springs Road

Round trip: 9.5 miles*
Elevation range: 8316–11,021 feet
Difficulty: Difficult
Hiking time: 6 hours or overnight for a backpacking trip
Best canine hiking seasons: Spring through fall
Under foot and paw: Gravel, rock, and dirt
Regulations: Dogs must be on a leash 6 feet long or less. Waste must be removed and disposed of properly.
Map: USGS La Madre Spring and Griffith Peak 7.5' quadrangles
Information: United States Forest Service, Spring Mountains National Recreation Area, (702) 515-5400 and (in emergencies) (702) 872-5306, or *www.fs.fed.us/r4/htnf/districts/smnra/index.shtml*
Water available: No

*A high-clearance vehicle is needed to get to the trailhead

Getting there: Take US Highway 95 north out of Las Vegas. 5.4 miles past the Ann Road exit, take Nevada Highway 157 west toward Mount Charleston. Follow Nevada Highway 157 up to Kyle Canyon. Turn left onto Harris Springs Road (dirt road) after 12.5 miles. Follow Harris Springs Road for 3 miles until the road forks. Continue to the right for another 5.5 miles until you reach a parking area.

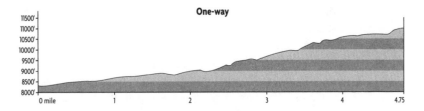

This hike is one where you can really get out and hike without meeting many people. This trail passes rocky areas, dense trees, meadows, and a high mountain peak. The fun for you and your pet is the time alone, varied landscape, and an abundance of incredible views. Griffith Peak is also accessible from the Kyle Canyon Lodge area, but this trail is much less traveled and gives you and your pet some privacy. Be aware that the Harris Springs Road is slow going. It takes a great deal of time to get back to the parking area, and a high-clearance vehicle is necessary. There are some sharp rocks on the road so be sure to have your spare tire along. This road is very windy, so if your dog gets carsick you may want to ask your veterinarian about motion sickness pills for your dog before setting out on this trek.

At the parking area, begin the hike along the old dirt road to the west. The Civilian Conservation Corps built this road in the 1930s. During the construction in 1935, President Roosevelt came out to inspect the work being done after his dedication speech at Boulder (Hoover) Dam. He asked where the road was going to end, and the supervisor couldn't answer, so the president stopped all work. It is for this reason that the

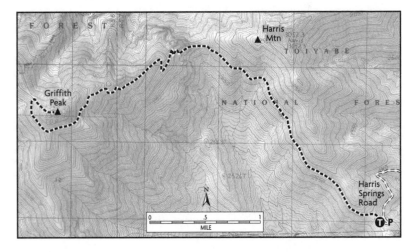

The hike always begins in smiles.

road abruptly ends and becomes a trail continuing from there.

After leaving the old road, the trail becomes steeper as it continues to the northwest. The terrain changes from pine forest to meadows, and eventually to bristlecone pines as you increase in elevation. Some dogs love playing in the tall grasses of meadows. If yours is one, definitely stop and play. As you near Griffith Peak, the designated trail stays on the south side and continues past the peak to the South Loop trail. Follow the established trail to the top of the peak from the west side for a west-to-east ascent. There are other trails leading up to the peak, but this trail is the most worn. Erosion and habitat disruption are kept to a minimum by staying on established trails, not blazing our own trail.

On the top of the peak, the 360-degree views are astounding! It is a great spot for viewing the surrounding region, and it would be worthwhile to bring your camera. Griffith Peak was named after Senator E.W. Griffith, who developed a resort area in Kyle Canyon. The terrain at Griffith Peak hosts an alpine plant community. The extreme elevation and weather conditions enable alpine plants to thrive. These plants tend to have quick life cycles and grow low to the ground. It is possible to have snow on the mountain far into the spring months, so be prepared for cool conditions. Typically, the conditions at the peak are cool and windy, so take some pictures and head downslope for a more protected resting spot. If your dog gets cold easily, you may want to pack a little doggie sweater to keep your pup warm. Return the way you came.

40. Mary Jane Falls

Round trip: 2.8 miles

Elevation range: 7843–8727 feet

Difficulty: Moderate

Hiking time: 3 hours

Best canine hiking seasons: Spring through fall

Under foot and paw: Gravel and dirt

Regulations: Dogs must be on a leash 6 feet long or less. Waste must be removed and disposed of properly.

Map: USGS Charleston Peak 7.5' quadrangle

Information: United States Forest Service, Spring Mountains National Recreation Area, (702) 515-5400 and (in emergencies) (702) 872-5306, or *www.fs.fed.us/r4/htnf/districts/smnra/index.shtml*

Water available: Two waterfalls

Getting there: Take US Highway 95 north out of Las Vegas. 5.4 miles past the Ann Road exit, take Nevada Highway 157 west toward Mount Charleston's Kyle Canyon area. Follow Nevada Highway 157 up to Kyle Canyon. Roughly 3 miles past the Kyle Canyon Visitor Center, Nevada Highway 157 will make an extreme left turn and an adjoining road will continue straight ahead into a residential area. Instead of following the

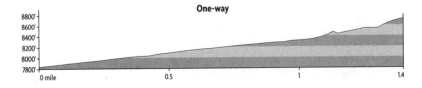

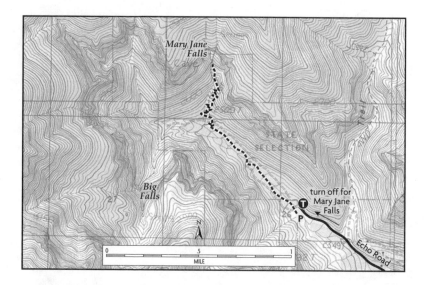

highway to the left, continue straight onto Echo Road. After 0.4 mile, turn left onto a dirt road that is marked Mary Jane Falls Parking Lot. Travel down the dirt road and park at the parking lot at the end.

Mary Jane Falls is an extremely popular hike, for people and dogs alike. Don't be surprised if you see several groups of hikers, all with dogs. The main draws to this hike are the waterfalls and the fact that the hike is only 2.8 miles (within that distance, you climb approximately 884 feet). For an added bonus, there is plenty of shade along the trail where everyone can catch their breath and relax.

The hike begins at the far end of the parking lot, immediately to the right of an information board and restroom. The trail begins on an old abandoned road with large rocks lining either side. In 1994, a large flood swept through the stands of aspen and ponderosa pine. Afterward, the Spring Mountains Youth Camp (SMYC) built the trail that you see today. The trail slowly ascends uphill through ponderosa pine, white fir, aspen, and mountain mahogany. After approximately 0.75 mile, the trail turns to the right where a series of switchbacks lead up the hillside toward a limestone cliff. Here, the trail gets much steeper, gaining approximately 500 feet over the next 0.65 mile. Make sure to stay on the trail throughout the ascent. Between the switchbacks are netting, chains, and rocks, used to help prevent erosion. Staying on the trails will keep you and your dog safer as well as aiding in the prevention of

Incredible views from Mary Jane Falls

erosion. The last thing you want is for your dog to get its little paws tangled in the netting.

The switchbacks and elevation change account for the moderate difficulty of this hike. There are many shaded areas along the trail, and downed logs and rocks provide places to sit and catch your breath while enjoying the scenery. It is always pleasant to take a moment to enjoy the difference of temperature and scenery at Mount Charleston compared to the Vegas valley floor. However, if you hike this trail often you will not be able to sit and rest for too long, because your dog will be pulling at the leash to get to the waterfalls at the top.

Farther up the trail, you reach the base of a large and impressive limestone cliff. Continue uphill along the base of the cliff. There is a series of stepping stones strategically placed along the trail to make your climb easier and to help prevent erosion. At the end of the trail there are two prominent year-round waterfalls cascading off the cliffs above. More water flows in early spring due to snowmelt, making the falls their most spectacular during this time. At the base of the two falls is a large open area with an expansive view facing southwest. This is a very popular spot for picnics and relaxing. More than likely, there will be other people and dogs enjoying the area. Ask the other dog owners if their dogs are friendly, and let the dogs socialize, play, and splash in the water. The mountain peak straight ahead is Charleston Peak, which stands at an impressive 11,918 feet. Also visible from the base of the falls is Big Falls across the canyon. Once done enjoying the area, return along the same trail to your car. It's all downhill this time!

41. Mummy Springs

Round trip: 5.7 miles
Elevation range: 8401–9983 feet
Difficulty: Moderate
Hiking time: 3.5 hours
Best canine hiking seasons: Spring through fall
Under foot and paw: Dirt trail
Regulations: Dogs must be on a leash 6 feet long or less. Waste must be removed and disposed of properly.
Map: USGS Charleston Peak and Angel Peak 7.5' quadrangles
Information: United States Forest Service, Spring Mountains National Recreation Area, (702) 515-5400 and (in emergencies) (702) 872-5306, or *www.fs.fed.us/r4/htnf/districts/smnra/index.shtml*
Water available: Spring

Getting there: Take US Highway 95 north out of Las Vegas. 5.4 miles past the Ann Road exit, take Nevada Highway 157 west toward Mount Charleston's Kyle Canyon area. Follow Nevada Highway 157 up to Kyle Canyon. Turn right onto Nevada Highway 158, which is also named Deer Creek Road. As you drive to the trailhead, carefully look up the hillside

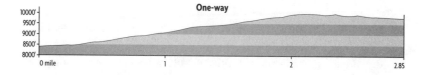

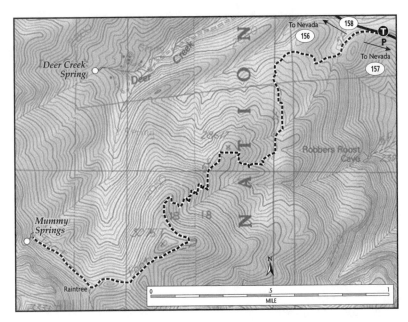

to the west (left). The Robber's Fire burned here in the summer of 2004. After 4 miles, park on the left side of the road in the parking area.

Mummy Springs is a protected, wooded area with a small spring and subsequent seasonal stream that your dog will love hiking to. The area is quite tranquil and has views of the Sheep Mountain Range to the northeast. The trail is well marked and straightforward with some switchbacks as you gain altitude, but overall quite moderate. "Raintree," the famous bristlecone pine tree, is along the route, just before Mummy Springs. The dogs will enjoy the terrain of this hike. The ground is primarily dirt, so it is easy on the paws. Regardless of what size your dog is—tall legs or short—as long as your dog is in shape it shouldn't have a problem on this trail.

The trailhead for this hike is at the parking area and is quite obvious. During the beginning of the trail there are occasional views off to the southwest of Kyle Canyon and beyond. Farther uphill to the southwest, the trail begins to switchback as it gains elevation. This is the most difficult portion of the hike. After the switchbacks, the trail levels out and you and your dog will be hiking in a bristlecone pine forest. These pines are ancient, up to thousands of years old. The trees are fairly small for a pine tree, with twisted golden-brown trunks.

After 2.5 miles, the Mummy Springs Trail comes in from the northwest (right). At the juncture is a very large bristlecone pine. This tree is known by the name "Raintree," and is one of the largest of its kind in this mountain range. The springs and associated mountain were named "Mummy" because the rock formation overlooking the area looks vaguely like a mummy. Quite frequently there is a nice breeze blowing at Raintree. If you and your dog are ready for a rest, on the south side of Raintree a wind block has been built. Throw your backpack down, lean up against it, and give your dog a few dog biscuits. There are many sticks lying around, so if your dog is up for a little game of fetch (when aren't they?), play fetch while resting by Raintree. From Raintree, lead your dog to the right and hike 0.3 mile to Mummy Springs.

The spring itself comes in from the left near a rock face. The runoff from the spring creates a small stream. The lush growth around the

Mummy Mountain is clearly visible from the trail.

stream, called the riparian zone, is extremely important in soil stabilization and nutrient uptake. Currently this area is under reclamation to allow the damaged riparian zone to repair. There are signs limiting access and redirecting hikers in the area. Please follow the direction of these signs to enable this ecosystem to recover. After enjoying this peaceful area with your dog, return the way you came.

42. North Loop Trail at Highway 158 to Trail Canyon Trail

Round trip: 11.6 miles*
Elevation range: 7925–9887 feet
Difficulty: Difficult
Hiking time: 6.5 hours
Best canine hiking seasons: Spring through fall
Under foot and paw: Dirt and gravel
Regulations: Dogs must be on a leash 6 feet long or less. Waste must be removed and disposed of properly.
Map: USGS Angel Peak and Charleston Peak 7.5' quadrangles
Information: United States Forest Service, Spring Mountains National Recreation Area, (702) 515-5400 and (in emergencies) (702) 872-5306, or *www.fs.fed.us/r4/htnf/districts/smnra/index.shtml*
Water available: Spring with a 0.3-mile detour to Mummy Springs

*5.8 using two cars, one parked at each end of the trail; hiking time 3.5 hours, moderate

Getting there: Take US Highway 95 north from Las Vegas. 5.4 miles past the Ann Road exit, take Nevada Highway 157 west, and head up the hill. Turn right onto Route 158, which is also named Deer Creek Road. After 4

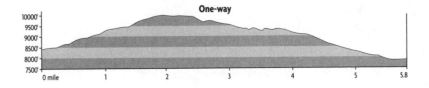

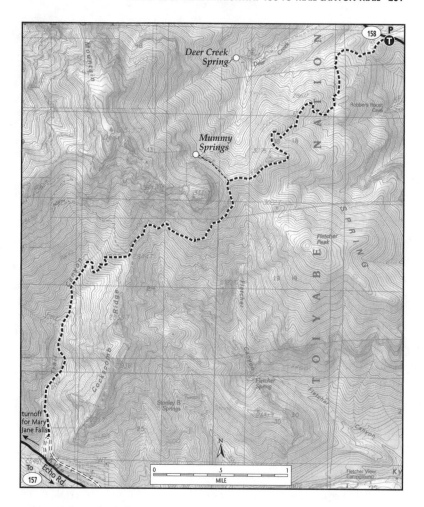

miles, park on the left in the parking area. For the one-way hike, park one vehicle here and the other at the Trail Canyon trailhead; see Cave Springs via Trail Canyon (Hike 37) for directions.

Probably the most stunning thing about this trek is its beautiful views. Throughout the hike there are panoramic views that can take your breath away. The high altitude keeps this hike a cool one, so pack an extra layer along in case you need it. The dogs will enjoy the shade and cool temperatures. This hike can be done as a long round-trip hike. For a 5.8-mile one-way downhill hike, use two cars, one parked at each end of the trail.

The trail begins at the parking area. This trail, called the North Loop

Summer is a great time to explore Mount Charleston.

trail, is a portion of the trail leading to the peak of Mount Charleston. The trek to the peak is a very strenuous 10.3-mile hike. This peak, originally named Nüvant or Snow Mountain, is significant in the mythology of the Southern Paiute. In 1869, a team of U.S. Army engineers named the peak after Charleston, South Carolina. Please note: This hike begins at the same trailhead as Mummy Springs (Hike 41), and the first portion of the trail is the same as for Mummy Springs.

From the trailhead, the trail is fairly level at first, but then it switchbacks to gain elevation. Shortly after the switchbacks is a bristlecone pine forest that is breathtaking. Mummy Mountain is visible rising up above the trail from this point. After 2.5 miles, the Mummy Springs trail comes in from the right. The springs are 0.3 mile down this trail, so if you have a dog that loves the water you may want to take this side route.

Continuing on the main trail, the way winds back and forth and up and down through a multitude of pines that provide shade throughout the hike. After passing the Mummy Springs trail, the hike generally heads downhill. There are many areas suitable for lunch or a quick doggy snack. To the north (right) is Mummy Mountain, and to the south there are great views of Griffith Peak (Hike 39) and Cathedral Rock (Hike 36). As you enjoy the views, your dog is going to love trotting down trail to see what is around the next curve. The trail is very well groomed and the dirt is soft, so there is nothing to distract your dog from eagerly pulling you downhill.

About 1.3 miles past the intersection with Mummy Springs, the trail approaches the northern tip of Cockscomb Ridge. The ridge is rather predominant due to its size. It will be to the south of the trail (left). At this point, the North Loop trail intersects the Trail Canyon Trail. Continue downhill on the trail to the trailhead and parking area. If you parked a second car here, head on home. If not, retrace your steps back uphill to your car.

VALLEY OF FIRE STATE PARK

The Valley of Fire State Park is well-known for its scenic beauty, fascinating geologic formations, and archaeological sites. On Easter Sunday in 1934, the Valley of Fire was dedicated as Nevada's first state park, with 8870 acres set aside for the preservation of its unique qualities. When you visit the park for the first time, you will understand why the park is so highly valued and how it got its name. The road into the park is flanked by red sandstone hillsides that jut out from the contrasting and seemingly stark desert landscape. When the sunlight hits the hillsides at just the right angle, the valley almost looks like it is on fire.

Adding to the beautiful scenery, the geologic formations of the Valley of Fire are the first things that grab your attention. The red sandstone found throughout the park is Aztec sandstone, the same type of sandstone found at Red Rock Canyon National Conservation Area. The hillsides throughout the Valley of Fire are actually ancient sand dunes formed when dinosaurs roamed the area approximately 150 million years ago. Geologic faults in the region caused uplifting and brought these rocks to the surface. Extensive erosion caused by wind and rain created the landscape you see today. Other important rock formations found throughout the park include limestones, shales, and conglomerates. As you explore the park, there are several places to stop and learn more about the geology: Arch Rock, Beehives, Fire Canyon/Silica Dome, Rainbow Vista, and Seven Sisters.

Possibly attracted by the scenery and beauty, people occupied the Valley of Fire region from approximately 300 BC to AD 1150. Prehistoric users included the Basket Maker people and, later, the Anasazi Pueblo, who also farmed in the nearby Moapa Valley. Since there is no reliable supply of water here, it is thought that these prehistoric peoples limited their time here to hunting, food gathering, and religious ceremonies. There are several places throughout the park where you can see petroglyphs—ancient rock art—left by these peoples. Later people who made their mark on the

Valley of Fire included Captain John J. Clark, an infantryman who died here in 1915; the Civilian Conservation Corps; and the users and creators of the Arrowhead Trail, an all-weather route that once ran between Los Angeles and Salt Lake City. To see remnants of these historical user groups, visit Atlatl Rock, the Cabins, Clark's Memorial, Mouse's Tank, and the Arrowhead Trail (Hike 43).

An important thing to remember when setting out on an adventure in the Valley of Fire is the temperature. During the summer, the average daily temperature at the park usually exceeds 100°F, and it often reaches 120°F. During the winter, temperatures can be mild, but they can also reach below freezing. For this reason, it is advisable to hike at the Valley of Fire in the spring, fall, and on mild winter days. Make sure you never leave your dog in the car when the weather is warm. Temperatures in a closed-up car skyrocket quickly, and your dog's health may be at risk if left under these circumstances.

Please note: The Valley of Fire State Park requires a fee for entrance. The entrance fee for a car is $6.00, and an annual pass can be purchased for $60.00.

43. Arrowhead Trail

Round trip: 1.15 miles
Elevation range: 1740–1866 feet
Difficulty: Easy
Hiking time: 1 hour
Best canine hiking seasons: Fall through spring
Under foot and paw: Sand, gravel, and a metal bridge
Regulations: Fee area. Dogs must be on a leash 6 feet long or less.
Waste must be removed and disposed of properly.
Map: USGS Valley of Fire East 7.5' quadrangle
Information: Valley of Fire State Park, (702) 397-2088
(Note: If calling from Las Vegas, you must dial the area code),
or *www.parks.nv.gov/vf.htm*
Water available: No

Getting there: From Las Vegas, take Interstate 15 north to exit 75, Valley of Fire and Lake Mead (23.5 miles past the exit for the 215 Beltway). Turn east (right) off the exit ramp, pass the Moapa Paiute Travel Plaza, and follow

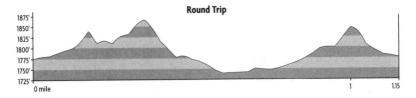

Nevada Route 169 for about 14.5 miles to the Valley of Fire State Park fee booth. From the fee booth, continue driving 7 miles to the east entrance area, which is on the north (left) side of the road. There is a parking lot and information kiosk. Park here. This is the trailhead.

The Arrowhead Trail is a short loop that takes you and your dog between two red sandstone hillsides to a great view of the open desert valley, and then to Elephant Rock, a popular rock formation. You and your doggie will enjoy this hike because you get to experience quite a bit in a short distance, which leaves no time for boredom. If you are new at hiking and are not confident in your ability to follow a trail without getting lost, this trail is extremely well marked, so give it a try.

From the parking lot, the trail begins on the north side of the information kiosk. There is a sign directly behind the kiosk showing that Elephant Rock and the Arrowhead Trail lead off to the left. Follow the

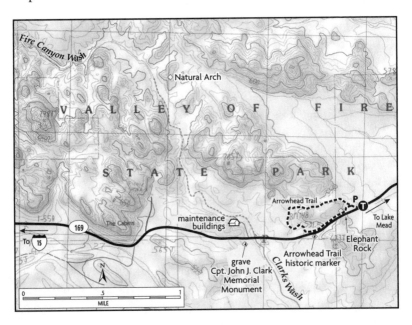

Jennifer takes a break on the bridge with her friends.

trail to the left. After about 0.1 mile, there will be another sign with an arrow pointing straight ahead for the Arrowhead Trail, and left for Elephant Rock. Follow the trail straight ahead; on the return portion of the loop, the trail will pass Elephant Rock.

Just past the sign, the trail begins to gain a little altitude as it curves around the backside of the hillside and leads you between two ridges of red sandstone. Wind and rain have eroded the hillsides down to their current shape, and in places the crevices that have been created are very interesting. The ground for this portion of the trail is primarily sand with some small gravel-sized rocks, so it should be easy on your dog. If there is a crevice in the sandstone that interests you, by all means take your dog to it and investigate.

After about 0.38 mile, the trail emerges from the sandstone ridges and a wide view of the valley opens up before you. The trail then turns to the south (left) and heads back downhill toward the road. About 0.6 mile into the hike, the trail intersects an old dirt road and begins to head east, back in the direction of your parked car. Shortly after the trail meets up with the dirt road, there is a metal bridge that crosses over a wash. Pay close attention to your dog here—some dogs may be unsure about crossing the bridge. If your dog refuses, find a safe place to cross on either side of the bridge. From the bridge, the trail parallels the main road, in several places getting awfully close to it. Make sure to keep your dog close and under control to eliminate a dangerous situation. At one point, the trail becomes the shoulder of the road; then it turns left and heads back downhill to complete the loop. Before heading downhill, look up above you to see the Elephant Rock formation. Many people say this rock looks like the head of an elephant with its big ears and long trunk reaching down. If your dog likes rock scrambling, there is a trail leading up the hillside to the base of the formation.

From Elephant Rock, continue down the trail and complete the loop. It may be tempting to just walk back to your car along the road, but for the safety of your dog this is not recommended.

44. Charlies Spring and Beyond

Round trip: 6.9 miles
Elevation range: 1406–1691 feet
Difficulty: Moderate
Hiking time: 3.5 hours
Best canine hiking seasons: Fall through spring
Under foot and paw: Gravel and dirt
Regulations: Fee area. Dogs must be on a leash 6 feet long or less. Waste must be removed and disposed of properly.
Map: USGS Valley of Fire East 7.5' quadrangle
Information: Valley of Fire State Park, (702) 397-2088
   (Note: If calling from Las Vegas, you must dial the area code), or *www.parks.nv.gov/vf.htm*
Water available: Spring

Getting there: From Las Vegas, take Interstate 15 north to exit 75, Valley of Fire and Lake Mead (23.5 miles past the exit for the 215 Beltway). Turn east (right) off the exit ramp, pass the Moapa Paiute Travel Plaza, and follow Nevada Route 169 for about 14.5 miles to the Valley of Fire State Park fee booth. From the fee booth, continue driving 6.1

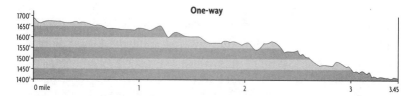

miles to the historic marker for Captain John J. Clark. The marker will be on the right side of the road, just past a white cross that is down in the wash to the right. Park your vehicle off the road near the historic marker sign. This is the trailhead.

The diversity of this hike keeps it fun and entertaining for dogs as well as their owners. The beginning portion of the hike has historical significance, with a memorial. From there it's off to a wide wash, then some sandstone scrambling. Then the fun part—water! There is enough water here to splash around in and let your dog get its feet wet. This wash is also not often hiked, so you and your pet will likely be alone.

The trail starts at the historic marker's information kiosk. This wash was named after Captain John J. Clark, a retired infantryman who died in this spot while traveling through the area. From the kiosk, the memorial is visible to the west. The memorial is a white brick structure with a large white cross on the top. "Clark" is engraved at the base of the memorial.

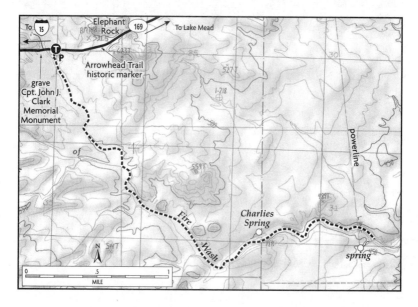

From the memorial, hike down the wash to the south. This is a typical desert wash with the occasional cat claw acacia and desert willow, and a host of desert scrub bushes. After 1.08 miles, this wash joins in with a much larger one from the west. From here the wash is very wide, with beautiful sandstone formations along the east wall. In wet seasons, there is fine, short green grass that grows along the bushes. The sharp contrast of the green next to the gray wash gravel is striking.

After another mile, watch out! Change is in the air! This large wash narrows and the walls and floor of the wash become bright red sandstone. This is the toughest portion of the hike and requires a small amount of scrambling. The scrambling is easy and, for most mutts, quite fun!

As you continue down the wash, the dogs will enjoy the water that begins to seep from the ground and forms a small stream. This area is great for doggie splashing and acting silly. This stream is created by what's known as Charlies Spring.

From here continue down the wash, enjoying the stream along the way. Due to the presence of water, this wash is widely used by the surrounding wildlife. It is not uncommon to see burros or bighorn, or at least signs

Bailey enjoys scrambling up the sandstone.

that these critters have been here. Remember to watch your dog carefully if you should stumble upon any of these large mammals. The encounter can be frightening for both your dog and the wild animal.

During wet seasons this area can be quite wet, with many little streams running their courses downhill. In fact, this area can get downright muddy—perfect for those dogs that love to get a little dirty on their hikes.

Continuing down the wash, watch for a utility line crossing the wash overhead. Shortly afterward, there will be a small drainage from the south (right). This area also flows with water and is quite lush with thickly growing, water-loving plants. This water is a little harder to enjoy due to the dense growth, but the small waterfall and subsequent stream where the drainage meets the wash can be quite fun for splashing around.

After your dog has had his fill of water play, return the way you came.

45. Natural Arch

Round trip: 2.8 miles
Elevation range: 1673–1782 feet
Difficulty: Easy
Hiking time: 1–2 hours
Best canine hiking seasons: Fall through spring
Under foot and paw: Primarily sand with one set of boulder-sized rocks
Regulations: Fee area. Dogs must be on a leash 6 feet long or less. Waste must be removed and disposed of properly.
Map: USGS Valley of Fire East 7.5' quadrangle
Information: Valley of Fire State Park, (702) 397-2088 (Note: If calling from Las Vegas, you must dial the area code), or *www.parks.nv.gov/vf.htm*
Water available: No

Getting there: From Las Vegas, take Interstate 15 north to exit 75, Valley of Fire and Lake Mead (23.5 miles past the exit for the 215 Beltway). Turn east (right) off the exit ramp, pass the Moapa Paiute Travel Plaza, and follow Nevada Route 169 for about 14.5 miles to the Valley of Fire State Park fee booth. From the fee booth, continue driving 6.1 miles to the historic marker for John J. Clark. The marker is on the right side of the road, just

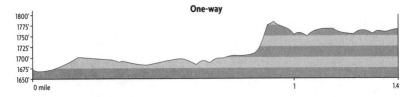

past a white cross that is down in the wash to the right. Park your vehicle off the road near the historic marker sign. This is the trailhead.

The Natural Arch hike is one of the simplest and most pleasant hikes described in this book. The trail follows a wide wash, with the finest red sand, to a picturesque natural arch. People enjoy this trail for the beauty of the sandstone hillsides, the solitude, and the arch found at the end of the trail. Dogs enjoy this trail for the sand. It is unquestionably the finest, softest sand found anywhere around Las Vegas. If your dog loves to roll in, dig in, or even eat sand (yes, some dogs are just that crazy), you would be doing your four-legged friend a great disservice by not taking him hiking here.

From the historic marker, carefully lead your dog across to the north side of the road. As always, this can be the most dangerous part of the hike. Walk downhill to the west (left) toward the wash. This is the same

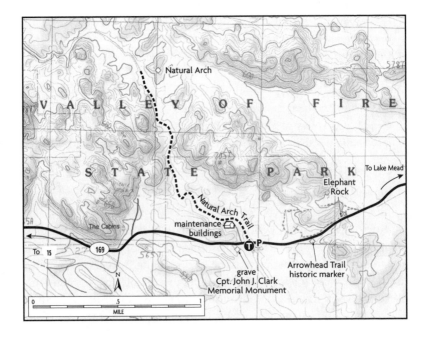

The Natural Arch is located high on the right side of the trail.

wash that has the white cross in it on the south side of the road. The wash is also distinguishable by the two large drainage channels that go under the road. As you walk down the hillside, watch out for tumbleweed growing in the disturbed areas. Tumbleweeds can be prickly, and have the potential to get stuck in your dog's coat. Once in the wash, follow it north. After a short distance, there are two buildings and a storage area on your left. These structures are pretty well hidden by vegetation, but you can see the power poles running to them. Pass the buildings and head up the wash.

This hike follows the wash in a northwestern direction through spectacular red sandstone formations. For most of the hike, the trail is wide and, toward the beginning of the hike, lined with mesquite trees. Just short of one mile into the hike, the trail narrows and there are two rocky areas that you must climb over. For most dogs, these areas should not be difficult to navigate. If you have a short-legged dog, you may need to lift it up and over the obstacles. After the first rocky area, which is kind of like a slippery, rocky slide, the trail curves around to the left toward a second boulder-like area to climb up. Just to the left of this spot is the neatest mini slot canyon. This slot canyon is the perfect size for dogs, but just a little bit too small for humans. Go ahead and let your dog explore it, your dog will think it's a blast!

Past the mini slot canyon, the trail opens back up to a wide wash. There are tall sandstone formations on both sides of the wash, but they are set back slightly. Look for the natural arch that this hike is named after when the sandstone formations on the right side of the wash butt up against the wash. The arch is at the top of the formation, a good 30-plus feet up above the wash. The bridge formation is thick on the left side and very thin on the right side. Immediately across from the wash is a small hillside. If you want a better view of the arch, perhaps for a photo, climb up onto the hillside.

The area around the arch is a great place for a picnic. If you brought a tennis ball or Frisbee with you, this is also a great place for a game of fetch. If you are interested in hiking farther, you can continue to follow the wash northwest. If you would like to return to your car, retrace your footsteps.

46. Pinnacles

Round trip: 4 miles
Elevation range: 2228–2572 feet
Difficulty: Moderate
Hiking time: 3 hours
Best canine hiking seasons: Fall through spring
Under Foot and Paw: Gravel and sand
Regulations: Fee area. Dogs must be on a leash 6 feet long or less. Waste must be removed and disposed of properly.
Map: USGS Valley of Fire West 7.5' quadrangle
Information: Valley of Fire State Park, (702) 397-2088
(Note: If calling from Las Vegas, you must dial the area code), or *www.parks.nv.gov/vf.htm*
Water available: No

Getting there: From Las Vegas, take Interstate 15 north to exit 75, Valley of Fire and Lake Mead (23.5 miles past the exit for the 215 Beltway). Turn east (right) off the exit ramp, pass the Moapa Paiute Travel Plaza, and follow Nevada Route 169 for about 14.5 miles to the Valley of Fire

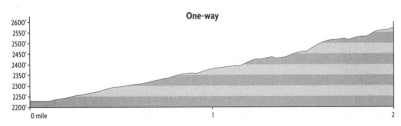

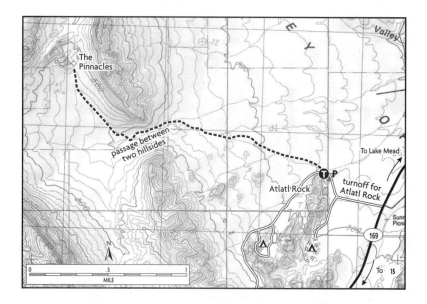

State Park fee booth. From the fee booth, continue driving 1.7 miles to the turnoff for Atlatl Rock, which will be on the left side of the road. Follow the signs to Atlatl Rock and park in the parking lot. The trailhead is directly across the road by the signs that point to the parking lot.

The Pinnacles Trail is a nice hike up a wash to a hidden outcrop of sandstone formations shaped like pinnacles. For most of the hike the pinnacles are hidden from view—it is a nice treat when you round the corner and they all stand in front of you. The trail is less known than many others in the park, so if peace and quiet are what you are looking for, this is the hike for you. Your four-legged friend will enjoy all the smells along the trail. Since there are not many people tromping up the wash, all the smells are the smells of nature—let your dog sniff around. Always remember to watch where your dog is sticking its snout. You never know when a rattlesnake may be resting under a plant or next to a rock.

After parking your vehicle in the parking lot, carefully lead your dog across the street by the stop sign. Walk in front of the sign pointing to Atlatl Rock, and continue to the large wash just beyond the sign. The wash will serve as the trail for this hike. Follow the wash to the west (left) toward two gray hills that have a passageway in between them. The hills are just beyond the sandstone outcrops on the south (left) side of the trail. Shortly into the hike, the wash forks. Follow the fork to the right.

The hike up the wash is slightly uphill, and the wash floor is gravelly, with small-to-medium-sized rocks throughout. The path of the wash may change a bit from season to season, as storms alter the wash floor. As the wash winds around, try and stay in the main portion of the wash heading for the split in the hillside instead of taking one of the small offshoots. The wash is lined fairly densely with desert shrubs and you know what that means: lizards must be hiding in there! Does your dog like to chase lizards and circle a shrub, convinced there is something in there? There will be plenty of opportunities for lizard-chasing along this wash.

As you hike toward the hillside, notice the sandstone outcrops on the south side of the trail. The trail begins to pass them about 0.5 mile into the hike. The sandstone outcrops are beautiful shades of orange, white, and red. After about 0.75 mile from the parking lot, the trail passes the last large sandstone outcrop, a yellow formation just on the south side of the wash. Make special note of this formation because you will want to use it as a landmark on your return trip.

Approximately 1.3 miles into the hike, you and your dog will pass through the opening between the hillsides. The wash swings around to the right and hugs the northern hillside. At this point, the trail does not seem to be leading anywhere exciting. All you will see is an open bowl

Mollie and Camy practicing their "Sit-Stay."

area, surrounded by mountains. As you pass through the hillsides, there is a lot of brush, so try to stay in the wash that hugs the hillside to the right. As you round the corner, you can see the Pinnacles directly in front of you. This is where the trail starts to get more exciting since you can finally see the destination. Continue following the wash to the Pinnacles. Let your dog explore the sandstone formations, and maybe enjoy your lunch if you packed one.

On the return trip to the car, after you and your dog pass through the opening between the hillsides, try to stay in the wash to the right. Direct your dog to the yellow sandstone outcrop on the south side of the wash. If you end up in the wrong wash, just head cross-county to the yellow outcrop to get back on trail. Watch your step along the way, because there are cacti growing outside the wash. The wash immediately adjacent to the large yellow sandstone outcrop will lead you to the Atlatl parking lot.

47. Rainbow Vista Trail with a side trip to Fire Canyon Overlook

Round trip: 2.15 miles
Elevation range: 2165–2055 feet
Difficulty: Easy
Hiking time: 1 hour
Best canine hiking seasons: Fall through spring
Under foot and paw: Soft sand
Regulations: Fee area. Dogs must be on a leash 6 feet long or less. Waste must be removed and disposed of properly.
Map: USGS Valley of Fire West 7.5' quadrangle
Information: Valley of Fire State Park, (702) 397-2088 (Note: If calling from Las Vegas, you must dial the area code), or *www.parks.nv.gov/vf.htm*
Water available: No

Getting there: From Las Vegas, take Interstate 15 north to exit 75, Valley of Fire and Lake Mead (23.5 miles past the exit for the 215 Beltway). Turn east (right) off the exit ramp, pass the Moapa Paiute Travel Plaza, and follow Nevada Route 169 for about 14.5 miles to the Valley of Fire State

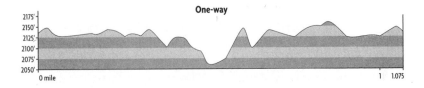

Park fee booth. From the fee booth, continue driving 7 miles and turn left onto the road leading to the visitor center. Just before the center, the road forks. Follow the fork to the left (the fork to the right leads to the visitor center). Follow this road (White Domes Road) for 1.75 miles to the Rainbow Vista parking lot, just beyond the Mouse's Tank–Petroglyph Wash parking area.

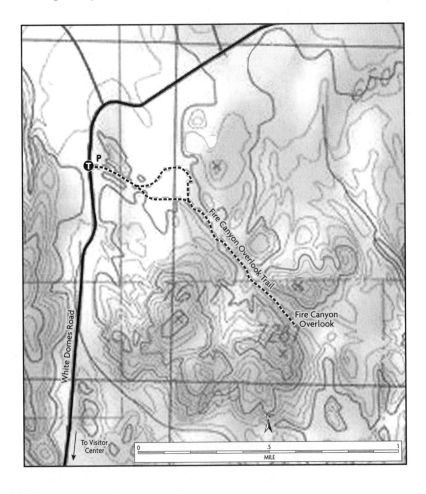

Bailey surveys the terrain of the Rainbow Vista Trail.

The Rainbow Vista Trail is a short loop among the sandstone. The Fire Canyon Overlook spurs off this trail to the southeast. This spur has fantastic views and is worth the extra walk.

If your dog loves sand, this is the place! The entire hike is on thick red sand, which is guaranteed to get into your socks and put a smile on your dog's face. This short, easy hike gives the dog owner some great views of fire-red and rainbow-colored sandstone. For dogs, this hike is nice and easy, and the sandy terrain keeps them interested and having fun.

The hike begins at the parking area. Follow the trail sign east from the parking area among the sandstone formations. Continuing from the parking area, look for a series of trail signs guiding the way to the hike. The trail begins by leading straight out into the desert.

After 0.2 mile the trail forks; continue straight ahead to the Fire Canyon Overlook. This portion of the hike has a little more uneven terrain, but is still an easy walk for most dogs. The sandstone formations narrow in on the trail, giving fantastic views of the curved, smooth sandstone pitted with holes. While you enjoy the views, let your dog explore the sandstone. The trail ends with a sign stating, "Fire Canyon Overlook Trail End." There are natural sandstone shapes that provide sitting spots. Take some time to relax here with your dog and take in the view of the fire-red shapes.

After your break, head back up the trail to the fork. This time, take the spur to the north (right). This part of the hike loops around in the desert among the sandstone formations, then back to the parking area. The sandstone here is much lighter in color than in the previous canyon. Some of the sandstone has bands of multiple colors similar to a rainbow. Again, follow the trail signs to keep on track. At the sign indicating a photo opportunity, stop and enjoy the views. From here, head back across the desert toward the parking area where you came in. Follow the wide track of footprints leading the way back to your vehicle.

48. White Dome Loop

Round trip: 1.1 miles
Elevation range: 1900–2119 feet
Difficulty: Easy
Hiking time: 1.5 hours
Best canine hiking seasons: Fall through spring
Under foot and paw: Soft sand, with some gravel and dirt
Regulations: Fee area. Dogs must be on a leash 6 feet long or less. Waste must be removed and disposed of properly.
Map: USGS Valley of Fire West 7.5' quadrangle
Information: Valley of Fire State Park, (702) 397-2088 (Note: If calling from Las Vegas, you must dial the area code), or *www.parks.nv.gov/vf.htm*
Water available: No

Getting there: From Las Vegas, take Interstate 15 north to exit 75, Valley of Fire and Lake Mead (23.5 miles past the exit for the 215 Beltway). Turn

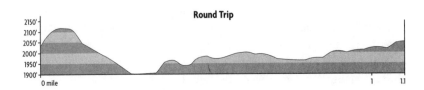

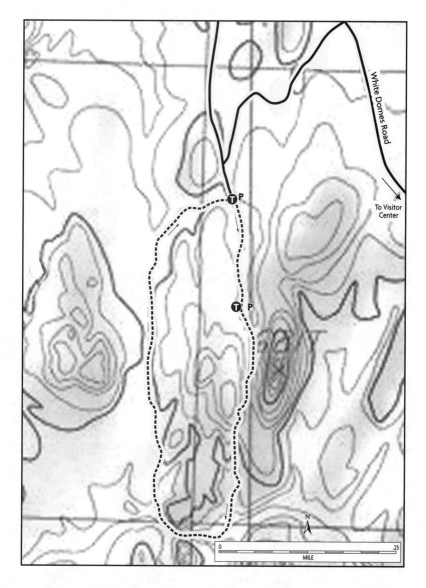

east (right) off the exit ramp, pass the Moapa Paiute Travel Plaza, and follow Nevada Route 169 for about 14.5 miles to the Valley of Fire State Park fee booth. From the fee booth, continue driving 7 miles and turn left onto the road leading to the visitor center. Just before the center, the road forks. Follow the fork to the left on White Domes Road (the fork to the right leads to the visitor center). Drive for 5.5 miles to the White Domes parking lot.

The White Domes area of the Valley of Fire looks like the landscape of another planet. On this hike, you and your dog will see rolling white sandstone outcrops, an old movie set, and a slot canyon. This short loop hike is a fun one for adults, kids, and dogs alike. While the hike is rather short, its diverse terrain makes it really enjoyable. Any dog should be able to hike this trail—even couch potato dogs!

The trailhead begins at the parking area near the restrooms and information plaques. The hike starts in and continues for some distance in sand. Expect sand in the shoes and some slick spots where sand covers hard rock surfaces. After 0.1 mile, the trail drops, moving down between two hills. In this area, the footing is often tricky across large rocks with a thin layer of sand on the surface. After 0.2 mile, the trail meets the remains of a movie set where *The Professionals* was filmed in 1966. There is an information plaque located near the set.

From the ruin, continue downhill on the trail until it runs perpendicularly into a wash. Follow the arrow sign and turn right following the wash. Shortly you will find a slot canyon, probably the most accessible slot canyon in the region. Slot canyons are narrow with very high walls formed by stormwater cutting through the relatively soft sandstone. Over time, the water cuts deeper and deeper until a canyon is formed. Canyons like this one can typically be shoulder-width wide, and hundreds of feet deep. (If you like slot canyons, see also Lovell Canyon, Hike 15). Slot canyons are cool due to the high canyon walls that provide shade. Your dog will love running through the curves to see what is on the other side.

After viewing a canyon like this, it is easy to see the strength and perseverance of stormwater. It is important to remember how destructive and potentially dangerous a flash flood can be to anyone caught in a slot canyon during a storm. The best defense is knowledge. Check out weather reports prior to hiking to find out if rain is forecast for the immediate and surrounding area.

Shortly after exiting the slot canyon, follow the arrow sign to the right uphill. From here the trail continues for some distance along the base of the hillside. Look around—in this area are some impressive sandstone formations. The trail winds around through open desert and eventually joins the road back to the parking area.

Opposite: Princess urges Paula to pick up the pace.

OTHER AREAS

T he following two hikes are not in an established park but on Bureau of Land Management land just on the outskirts of Las Vegas. Both hikes give views of the Las Vegas Valley, one from the west side and one from the east. With the continued growth in Las Vegas, hikes like these are interesting to hike regularly to see the growth and expanse of our ever-changing valley.

49. Frenchman Mountain

Round trip: 4 miles
Elevation range: 2400–3952 feet
Difficulty: Difficult
Hiking time: 3–4 hours
Best canine hiking seasons: Fall through spring
Under foot and paw: Old dirt road with rocky areas
Regulations: Dogs may be off leash, but must be under control. Waste, including but not limited to dog waste, must be removed and disposed of properly.
Map: USGS Frenchman Mountain 7.5' quadrangle
Information: Bureau of Land Management, Las Vegas Field Office, (702) 515-5000, or *www.nv.blm.gov*
Water available: No

Getting there: The Frenchman Mountain trailhead is located in the northeast corner of the Las Vegas Valley. Take Lake Mead Boulevard east toward Sunrise Mountain. One mile past Hollywood Boulevard, there is a historical site marker on the south side of the road. If you are interested in geology, take a quick stop here. The historical site marks the Great

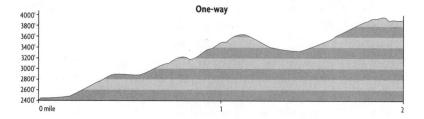

Unconformity, where rocks that are 1.7 billion years old are found layered next to rocks that are about 520 million years old. The rocks on the right side of the historical site are 1.7 billion-year-old Precambrian granite and schist. They formed deep within the earth in the core of an ancient mountain range. During hundreds of millions of years this old mountain range eroded away, leaving the rocks exposed about 500 million years ago. The rocks were then buried by sand when the area was covered by a shallow sea. The sand cemented together to form the sandstone seen to the left of the historical site. The buried erosion surface is the Great Unconformity, which represents about 1.2 billion years of missing history. The earth is about 4.5 billion years old, so this surface represents more than one-fourth of the earth's history.

From the Great Unconformity, continue driving on Lake Mead Boulevard another 1.1 miles, then turn right onto an unnamed dirt road. (The dirt road is just before a hard right turn with a 40-miles-per-hour speed limit sign.) Pull off onto the dirt road and continue straight ahead. The area immediately adjacent to the highway is often used for illegal dumping, so make sure you drive uphill a little ways past any trash that may be in the area before parking your car off to the side of the road. The trail follows the service road up the hillside.

Congratulations! You have just found one of the two hikes in this book where dogs are not required to be on leash. Frenchman Mountain is the tallest peak (4052 feet) on the east side of the Las Vegas Valley; it is frequently mistaken for Sunrise Mountain, but Sunrise is the shorter peak to the north. Frenchman Mountain is in an area managed by the Bureau of Land Management, but is not within a designated park or recreation area, so there are no regulations requiring dogs to be on leashes. However, if you do let your dog off leash, keep a close eye on your dog because there are often piles of trash dumped in the area, particularly in the vicinity of East Lake Mead Boulevard.

Although there are a couple of ways to get to the top of Frenchman Mountain, following the old rocky service road is your best bet when hiking with dogs. The alternative route has sharp rocks, an undefined trail, and a lot of cacti. The hike described here follows the service road to the top of Frenchman Mountain. To get the top, you must ascend two extremely steep hills, the second even steeper than the first. This service road makes an easy path to follow, even if your dog is running ahead.

The hike begins at the base of the first of the two hills. The first section of hill is a good warm-up climb about 0.4 mile long, with an elevation gain of about 450 feet. After getting to the top of this first hill, you will realize why it's the warm-up. The top of this hill is actually the base of another, dauntingly high hill. The next portion of the hike gains approximately 762 feet in about 0.75 mile. Along the way there is a black SUV that once tried to make it up the road, but rolled off the side into a gully. Keep your pet close, making sure your pooch does not go exploring the wreck, which may be unstable or have critters like rattlesnakes resting in the crevices of the warm metal. As you get closer to the top of the

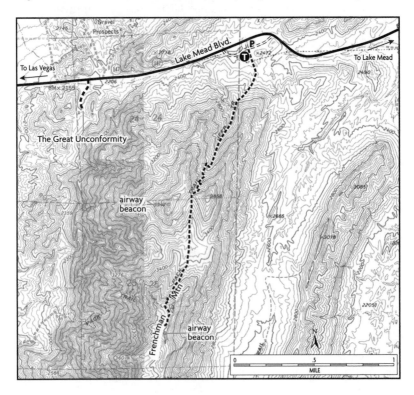

Mollie, Katia, and Camy at the top of Frenchman Mountain.

hill, the road makes several switchbacks before reaching the pinnacle. You may expect a great view of the Valley from the top, but not yet; you are only half-way there—at the top of the first hill.

From this vantage point of 3600 feet in elevation, you have your first glance at the second hill, an even taller one, and the peak of Frenchman Mountain. The mountain was named after a miner, Paul Watelet, who was actually Belgian, not French. In February 1912, Watelet declared he had found gold in the mountain. It is now thought that his "discovery" was actually a hoax.

The climb to the higher peak begins with a 0.4-mile walk down into a saddle, followed by an ascent to approximately 4000 feet in 0.6 mile. For many of us, this is a pretty steep grade, but for the dogs it doesn't seem like anything more than a run in the park. Dogs have the amazing ability to run ahead, come back and greet you, run ahead, come back and check on you again, then ascend to the top. In essence, they will climb the peak at least three times during our one ascent. It is simply amazing and gratifying at the same time, because we know they are going to sleep for the rest of the day once they get home.

From the top, the views are truly breathtaking. From the beautiful Mormon Temple directly below, to the strip, to Mount Charleston—you can see it all. While enjoying the view, let your dog take a rest. Return to your car by retracing your steps.

50. Lone Mountain

Round trip: 1 mile
Elevation range: 2775–3312 feet
Difficulty: Moderate
Hiking time: 1 hour
Best canine hiking seasons: Fall through spring
Under foot and paw: Dirt and rock
Regulations: Dogs may be off leash but must be under control. Waste, including but not limited to dog waste, must be removed and disposed of properly.
Map: USGS Blue Diamond 7.5' quadrangle
Information: Bureau of Land Management, Las Vegas Field Office, (702) 515-5000, or *www.nv.blm.gov*
Water available: No

Getting there: Lone Mountain is located on the northwest side of the Las Vegas Valley. Take US Highway 95 north from Las Vegas to Cheyenne Avenue. Turn west (left) over the highway and then turn north (right) on Tenaya. After 1 mile, turn west (left) onto Alexander. Drive 3.7 miles around the south side of Lone Mountain, past Jensen Road, and make a right on Vegas Vista Trail. Drive for 0.4 mile until the pavement ends, then continue for another 0.1 mile to an unpaved parking area on the right near the base of the mountain. Interstate 215 is visible from the parking area.

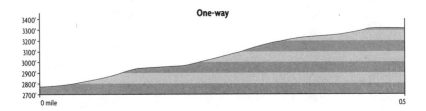

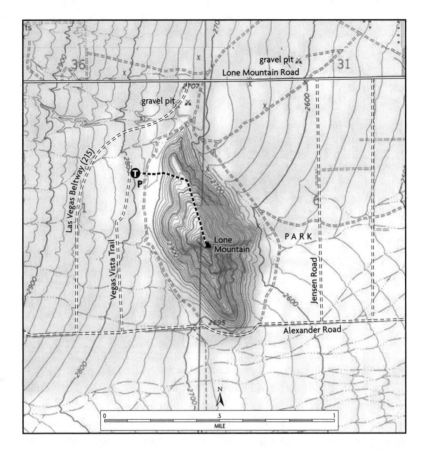

Located on the northwest side of the Las Vegas Valley, Lone Mountain juts out of the horizon as a prelude to the larger mountains to the west. This short hike is easily accessed from Las Vegas since it is in town, and would make a great evening hike or short weekend hike when the dogs are just itching to get out. The trail does have some loose terrain and quite an incline, so it may not be suitable for older dogs. The trail puts you at the top of Lone Mountain, so get ready for 360-degree views of the entire valley! This is one of only two hikes in this book where dogs are not required to be on leash. Since there can be many people in this area, at minimum make sure your dog is under control, with good response to voice commands.

The trail begins from the dirt parking area, heading right up the hillside, and is quite steep. This portion of the trail has some loose sections, so watch your footing and your dog's in this area. As you reach the crest of the ridge, you are treated with incredible views to the east and north.

Buddy and Missy recently started hiking.

To the left is a park bench for a little rest while you soak up the view.

The trail to the top of the mountain continues to the right. The trail comes in and out of view in this section, but continuing up gradient will get you to the top. From the top, the entire valley is visible. Just to the east of the mountain is Lone Mountain Park. The Las Vegas strip is also clearly visible, with the Stratosphere marking the general vicinity. Your dog is going to love scrambling up to the top of the mountain, and since it does not have to be on leash here, you may enjoy the hike a little more than usual, since you will not be pulled up the mountain while holding on to a leash.

Watch your dogs closely at the top of the mountain. The area is limited in space, with steep drop-offs on either side. The limestone rock of this mountain can be tough on paws as well, but those dogs that love to clamber and climb will not even see this as a challenge. After soaking in the view, return the way you came.

> *"I've an appointment with a dog about a walk."*
>
> —*J.J. Connington* (Four Defences, *Little, Brown, and Company, 1940*)

APPENDIX: RESOURCES

Websites About Dogs and Hiking

www.uberpest.50megs.com/doghikefaq.html
www.lovetheoutdoors.com/camping/Act/Hiking/Hikedog.htm
www.sierraclub.org/e-files/dog_hiking.asp

Dog Packs and Trail Supplies

www.activek9.com/dog-backpacks.html
www.drsfostersmith.com
www.greatoutdoorsdepot.com/canine-packs.html
www.granitegear.com
www.planetdog.com
www.rei.com
www.ruffwear.com
www.tailsend.com/productcart/pc/viewCat_h.asp?idCategory=9
www.wolfpacks.com

Books

Acker, Randy and Jim Fergus. *Field Guide: Dog First Aid Emergency Care for the Hunting, Working, and Outdoor Dog* (Field Guide). Wilderness Adventures Press, 1994.

Fogle, Bruce and Amanda Williams. *First Aid for Dogs: What to Do When Emergencies Happen.* (Reprint edition) Penguin Books, 1997.

Giffin, James M. and Lisa D. Carlson. *Dog Owner's Home Veterinary Handbook,* 3d ed. Howell Book House, 1999.

Hoffman, Gary. *Hiking with Your Dog: Happy Trails,* 3d ed. Mountain N' Air Books, 2002.

Kain, Tara. DogFriendly.com's *California and Nevada Dog Travel Guide,* 3d ed. DogFriendly.com, 2004.

Mullally, Linda. *Hiking with Dogs: Becoming a Wilderness-Wise Dog Owner.* Falcon Guides, 1999.

INDEX

ABOUT THE AUTHORS AND THE DOGS

Kimberly S. Lewis

Kimberly is an environmental planner with a private consulting company in Las Vegas, Nevada. Her knowledge of the desert began when she became a park ranger at Red Rock Canyon National Conservation Area, assisting with the environmental education program. Kimberly grew up hiking throughout California but now calls the desert her home. Kimberly has two dogs, Camy and Mollie. Camy was adopted from the SPCA, who rescued her in her last hour at a local kill shelter. She is a purebreed mutt, but if forced to guess she may be part Australian cattle dog. Mollie was rescued as well. Her previous owner dropped her and her sister off in the middle of the desert in the middle of the summer. Mollie and her sister were found and taken in by Noah's Ark Pet Rescue and later adopted from in front of a local pet store. Mollie is a border collie with perhaps a little sheltie mixed in.

Kimberly and her two hiking companions, Camy and Mollie

Paula M. Jacoby-Garrett

Paula is a research scientist at the University of Nevada, Las Vegas, and also teaches environmental science at the Community College of Southern Nevada. She began her writing career by self-publishing the book *Las Vegas Hiking Guide* (1997, currently out of print). Paula's wildlife-biologist husband, Bill, and their two children, Gwen and Evan, enjoy hiking and camping as much as possible. Paula and her family have three dogs. Jazmine is a 10-year-old German shepherd who has been a part of the Garrett household since she was five weeks old. Now partially blind, Jaz has to rely on verbal signals to keep her hikes safe, fun, and on the path. Princess is a two-year-old poodle and the silly puppy of the group. She is a social butterfly and feels it is her duty to welcome all those on the trail whether dog or human. Paula's "step" dog is Bailey, a five-year-old Shetland sheepdog and Paula's parents' dog. Bailey is a suburban girl who has just recently found the joys of desert hiking. Just before finishing this book, Paula and her family adopted CJ, a year-old male German shepherd, from a local animal rescue. CJ hasn't gotten a chance to go exploring the desert yet.

For more information about the authors and their dogs, visit *www. twodesertchicks.com.*

Paula with Bailey, Princess, and Jazmine